CULTURE SHOCK!

Scotland

Jamie Grant

Graphic Arts Center Publishing Company
Portland, Oregon

In the same series

Argentina	Denmark	Japan	South Africa
Australia	Ecuador	Korea	Spain
Austria	Egypt	Laos	Sri Lanka
Belgium	Finland	Malaysia	Sweden
Bolivia	France	Mauritius	Switzerland
Borneo	Germany	Mexico	Syria
Brazil	Greece	Morocco	Taiwan
Britain	Hong Kong	Myanmar	Thailand
California	Hungary	Nepal	Turkey
Canada	India	Netherlands	UAE
Chile	Indonesia	Norway	Ukraine
China	Iran	Pakistan	USA
Costa Rica	Ireland	Philippines	USA—The South
Cuba	Israel	Scotland	Venezuela
Czech Republic	Italy	Singapore	Vietnam

Barcelona At Your Door	New York At Your Door	A Traveler's Medical
Beijing At Your Door	Paris At Your Door	Guide
Chicago At Your Door	Rome At Your Door	A Wife's Guide
Havana At Your Door	San Francisco At Your	Living and Working
Jakarta At Your Door	Door	Abroad
Kuala Lumpur, Malaysia	Tokyo At Your Door	Personal Protection At
At Your Door		Home & Abroad
London At Your Door	A Globe-Trotter's Guide	Working Holidays
Moscow At Your Door	A Parent's Guide	Abroad
Munich At Your Door	A Student's Guide	

Illustrations by TRIGG
All photographs by Jamie Grant, with the exception of the one on page 113 by Ceara Conway
Front cover photograph by Dave G. Houser
Back cover photograph by Trip Photographic Library

© 2001 Times Media Private Limited
Revised 2003

This book is published by special
arrangement with Times Media Private Limited
Times Centre, 1 New Industrial Road, Singapore 536196
International Standard Book Number 1-55868-607-X
Graphic Arts Center Publishing Company
P.O. Box 10306 • Portland, Oregon 97296-0306 • (503) 226-2402

Printed in Singapore

To Simon Grant, whose memory still walks the tops of
Ben-y-Vrackie on a bright spring morning.

CONTENTS

ACKNOWLEDGMENTS

Thanks to Marcus, James, Maria, Dave, El, Suzie, Onya, Robin, Euan and Eveline—my friends and housemates by the Links. Special thanks to James for walking with me on a road less travelled, to Onya for her wicked turn of phrase and Marcus for keeping the humour flowing. I wish I could mention all the people who helped with my research but will have to settle for a special thanks to Paddy and Libby Shaw for their hospitality and wisdom, Penny Travlou for her insights and Roger Wood for getting me out of the rough. Thanks also to Nicolas Stepanopolus for giving me a place to rest on a long night and Jane and Ian for tying up loose ends with a few whiskies by the coal fire. Special thanks to Lucy, Charlie and Nigel as well as my new family, Roger, Jean and James. Love and kisses to my wife Fin, for being so unbelievably gorgeous.

SCOTLAND

SHETLAND
Shetland Islands
Vaila ● ● Lerwick

ORKNEY
Skara Brae ●
Mainland   *Orkney Islands*

● Stornoway
Lewis   ● Balallan
WESTERN
ISLES
North Uist
HIGHLAND
● Burghead
Drumnadrochit ●   Inverness ●
South Uist   Milton ●   ● Culloden   GRAMPIAN
Skye   ● Dornie   Loch
Ness
Highlands   ● Aberdeen
Cairngorms   *Dee*
Ben Nevis ▲   Balmoral
(4,406 ft/1,343 m)   ● Catterline
Moor of   TAYSIDE
Rannoch   ● Pitlochry
Loch Tay   Tay
Mull   Scone ● ▲ Dundee   *Dunsinane
Perth   (1,012 feet/308 m)*
ATLANTIC   CENTRAL ● Comrie   FIFE ● St. Andrews
Iona   Loch   *Central*
Katrine
Loch   ● Stirling ● Bannockburn   ● Prestonpans
Lomond
OCEAN   STRATHCLYDE   *Lowlands* ● Dunbar
Jura   Dunoon ●   ● Glasgow   EDINBURGH
LOTHIAN
Southern   Melrose ● *Tweed* ● Kelso
Uplands   BORDERS
DUMFRIES AND
GALLOWAY   *Cheviot Hills*
Gretna Green ●

NORTH

SEA

N

IRELAND

NORTHERN
IRELAND   ENGLAND

INTRODUCTION

"Land of polluted river
Bloodshot eyes and sodden liver
Land of my heart forever
Scotland the brave"
—Billy Connolly quoted in Jonathan Margolis,
The Big Yin (1994)

ANOTHER BOOK ON SCOTLAND...

Welcome to yet another book on Scotland! So much has been written
and rewritten on Scotland, Scottish life, its history and traditions that
you might think that any author today would throw up his hands and
say, "Enough is enough!" Yet somehow, Scotland continues to

inspire fascination and love amongst visitors and inhabitants alike. Sir Walter Scott's "land of brown heath and shaggy wood, land of the mountain and the flood," lives on in the hearts and imaginations of all those who go there.

This is a fine moment to take another look at a proud and increasingly confident people. After some three hundred years of political union with England, the Scots voted to have their own parliament in 1997.

The new millennium brings political devolution with an elected assembly now sitting in Edinburgh. This important step toward self-determination brings new hope and excitement for the future and greater vibrancy to the country and its people.

Scotland may remain part of Great Britain (England, Scotland, Wales, Northern Ireland), but it has always been a country apart. When you travel up from London on the train to Edinburgh or Glasgow you don't need signposts to tell you that you have arrived in a different environment. In England the countryside seems tempered and polished by time, the landscape neatly clipped and contained by centuries of overcrowding, over-farming, and zealous gardening. In contrast, Scotland's rifts, faults, and mountains seem to have been left in constant turmoil and revolt. The land and its people are truly different and in many ways seem rawer, younger, and less cynical.

Some 80% of the population live and work in the Central Belt, a broad swath of land that takes in Edinburgh, Glasgow and the 113 km (70 miles) or so in between. These two principal cities couldn't be more different. Edinburgh's stone facades, spires, and gothic alleyways have an elegant if austere charm about them. Glasgow, one of the great cities of the colonial empire, weaves Old World grandeur into a modern day metropolis. The weather also distinguishes Scotland's twin urban centres. Edinburgh is airier, blown as it is by a cold wind from the east, while Glasgow catches the rain that sweeps in from the west.

While the cities and towns of the densely populated southern part of Scotland are important and wonderful in their different ways, it is the character of the land itself that has such a profound effect on people. Southern Scotland is an undulating territory of hills and river valleys separated by the cold waters of the Solway Firth. Once the centre of a strong textile industry, young people in the Borders, Dumfries, and Galloway are now looking increasingly to the big cities for work.

Travel east out of Edinburgh and you're in the Kingdom of Fife, a peninsula of land running into the breakwaters of the North Sea with the town of St Andrews at its coastal tip. Although the landscape consists of flat and repetitive farmland compared to the Highlands, it still holds its own charm. Perhaps it's the string of old fishing villages that run all the way up to Wick in the north, a reminder of the days when the herring was king.

Travel up the coast and you'll reach Dundee and then Aberdeen. Aberdeen is the nation's third largest city and projects an oddly cosmopolitan image for a place so far north and so far away from the hub of things. Called the "Silver City" by locals, fishing, in areas such as Stonehaven, as well as crude oil have brought prosperity and work to this windswept environment.

Drive inland from Aberdeenshire and you reach mountain country. In the mad dash up to Loch Ness and the Isle of Skye, many tourists miss out on the Central Grampians and Perthshire. This is Scotland's geographical hub, a huge area that takes in much of the Highlands and the Lowlands to the east and the west. The landscape is a fantastic mix of woodlands, deep valleys, rivers, high moors, and mountains. In fact there is everything here but the sea.

To the north, Inverness is a hard-bitten Highland capital that provides much needed service jobs and industry to the region. The surrounding countryside is breathtaking. Then of course, is Loch Ness itself, a lake so dark and deep that just looking at it sends a chill through you. There are many other places that most visitors never see.

Hidden places like Glen Affric, where one of the last remnants of the old Caledonian forest can be found, or Loch Hourn, a spectacular sea loch situated on the west coast opposite Skye where the single track road ends at a tiny village.

Next to the far north, where cities and towns give way to narrow single track roads. It is here that you realise just how much of the country is open and uninhabited, one of the last wildernesses within Europe. Caithness in the Northeast is a wide plain where the northern light takes hold and the skies and oceans start to dominate these thinning lands. Farming and fishing still cling on in Caithness, particularly in the aptly named town of Wick. During winter, daylight in this northern town feels about as short as the last flame from an exhausted candle.

Run on down the west coast from Sutherland through Kinross, Argyle, and finally Ayrshire, and you will see some of the most spectacular views in Scotland, where the mountains run into ocean and cloud, and sunlight and rain are constantly moving and mixing. This is also the heart of an older, rural Scotland where salmon farming, shellfish, and crofting provide much of the employment.

Scotland isn't just the mainland north of England, it is also a multitude of islands separated by the sea. There are about 800 islands dotted around the mainland, about 130 of which are inhabited. People living on these watery fringes still hold on to many of the country's traditions and dialects. Most of the Gaelic-speaking communities are on islands along the west coast such as Harris and Lewis. The islands off the north and east coast, such as Orkney and the Shetlands, are old Pictish and Viking centres. It's not surprising that the Scandinavians have had such an influence on these islands since Shetland is actually closer to Oslo than London.

Scotland is a country of contrasts, a country dominated by its landscape and its weather, an odd mix of old and new. Spend a day in Glasgow and you can buy top designer clothes, drink frothy cappuccinos, go to the theatre, eat anything from fish and chips to a

Malaysian curry and dance the night away in a packed club. Travel three hundred miles north and you are in the magical seascape of the Orkney Isles, where there are so few cars that pedestrian crossings were only introduced in 1999.

Many of the stereotypes about Scotland and the Scots contradict the modern reality. The Scotland in brochures and travel guides of castles, romance, and battle sites means little to the majority of Scots who live in modern urban centres. Much of the big shipping and fishing industries of Scotland's proud industrial past have been reduced to old photos of stout men and women, baiting their long lines for the herring or beating out the vast steel bellies of ships.

Now in the spring of a political and cultural renaissance, the Scots are faced with the challenge of redefining themselves for the new millennium. Like the constant flow of weather and season in this magical northern land, the only certainty in Scotland is change. There couldn't be a more exciting time to come here.

A country as complex and multifaceted as Scotland cannot be squeezed into a single book, so I offer my apologies in advance for all the stories, places and people that I have been unable to include. They are still out there for you to meet and discover for yourself.

Chapter One

HISTORY IN RAINBOW COUNTRY

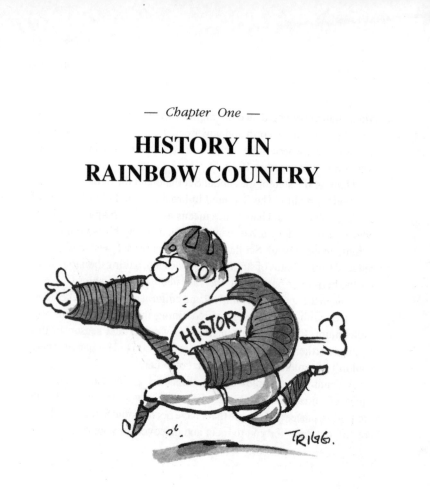

"Work as if you live in the early days of a better nation"
—Alasdair Gray, Scottish author.

What is it that draws people to Scotland? For many, Scotland's romantic image, carefully nurtured by its Tourist Board, sells the country and its people as a quaint tartan package. This image of "heritage Scotland" is self-evident in any tourist shop along the Royal

Mile in Edinburgh and now in most towns up and down the country. The image is of the picturesque Scotland of castles, kilts, whisky and of course the ubiquitous Loch Ness monster or "Nessie," which is sold in all guises, colours, and sizes—usually finished off with a tuft of ginger hair and a tartan cap.

Few in Scotland mind this quaint and well-marketed image as tourism supports some 177,000 jobs and fosters a unique image abroad that captivates the imagination. When travelling abroad I always know what to expect when I tell anyone I come from Scotland: "Oh yes, so you have a skirt then," (followed by much mirth) or "Ah yes, whisky please, whisky." An instant icebreaker!

The other common image of Scotland is of Scotland the Brave, brilliantly characterised by the now legendary film *Braveheart*. It is not that far from the actual historical events and follows the exploits of William Wallace (played by Mel Gibson). In the film a swashbuckling Wallace inflicts a series of crushing defeats on the English before coming to a sticky end. The real William Wallace ended up with his head on a spike on London Bridge, although the Scots have never lost his example of fighting spirit against the English.

The memory of a tartan army fighting off a numerically stronger foe, usually the English, still holds a lot of currency in Scotland. This legend of fierce independence and Scottish togetherness reached its tragic culmination in 1746 at Culloden, outside of Inverness. There, the Jacobite army of Highlanders, led by Bonnie Prince Charlie, were annihilated by English cannon and muskets (please turn to chapter nine for the details). The romantic notion of a single Scottish nation united in a single dream of independence may be at odds with the actual events of the time, but still remains in the minds of many.

The unified face of the Scots still comes out in force on the international rugby or football field, usually painted blue and white for the colours of the Caledonian flag. Here they sing for their nation with a single voice, regardless of whether the day ends in victory or honourable and spirited defeat.

As potent as these images of Scotland may be, they are more imagined than real. For anyone interested in Scotland and its people, disentangling the myth from the reality isn't easy. After all, myths are usually rooted in some truth.

The best place to start getting a better understanding of the Scots and their country is through their history not as a dry narrative but as a story that begins and ends with the present, the 21st century.

EARLY DAYS

The first link to early Scottish history lies in the landscape itself. As you travel through Scotland you constantly come across signposts to the past. Driving just north of the border with England, across the narrow waist of Scotland between the Forth and the Clyde rivers, you'll pass the remains of the Antonine Wall. Completed by the Romans in A.D. 142, it became their first line of defence against incessant waves of attack from midges, rain, and warring tribes, mainly the Picts, to the north. In the end the Romans beat a hasty retreat even further south, to Northumberland in England. Here they built the massive Hadrian's Wall and left Caledonia, or the "land of woods" as they then called Scotland, to its own devices.

Roman remains are only a fraction of the story. Pushing north through Perthshire a discerning eye can pick out prehistoric burial mounds and Iron Age hill forts dating from 500 B.C. Inconspicuous village graveyards point to a past long abandoned by living memory. In the small village of Moulin there is a 12th century crusader's grave, the outline of his double-handed broadsword chiselled into the stone. Whether he's one of the few crusaders who actually managed to fight their way into Jerusalem for Christianity only to be driven out by the Moors, is lost to everything but the imagination.

Another graveyard, this time in the village of Miegle, claims to hold the mound and stone of Lady Guinevere of Arthurian legend. This is a somewhat dubious claim—there is little real evidence of King Arthur, his round table of chivalrous knights or his unfaithful

An old Pictish settlement or "broch" near Glenelg on Scotland's west coast.

wife. Then again real life is often more fanciful than myth and for all we know, Guinevere could actually be buried there alongside the bones of her fickle and dashing knight, Sir Lancelot.

Glenelg boasts ancient stone structures known as *brochs*. These fortified dwellings were built by ancient Celtic settlers known as Picts. If you travel north to the Western Isles, you will find yourself in old Viking country, with the settlement remains of Jarlshof in Shetland and lurid graffiti on the even older burial site of Maes Howe in Orkney.

In January and February Shetlands locals still pay tribute to their Viking ancestors with two weeks of dancing and drinking in traditional pleated garb. Called the Up Helly Aa, this festival sees islanders marching through the town of Lerwick with torches and symbolically burning a mock-up of one of their ancestors' long ships.

Such remnants of Scotland's ancient settlers adds much to the country's mystique. The Pictish people were probably the first inhabitants of Scotland and survived until the 8th or 9th centuries A.D. All that we have left of them are the Brochs, a few settlement remains, and some wonderful carvings of both real and fanciful animals. The even older stone circles, such as Orkney's massive "Ring of Brodgar," are a complete enigma.

From these pointers to early Scottish history, the immense diversity of cultures and peoples that lived there already contradicts the image projected today of a single, homogenous Scotland. Whether it be medieval castles, Saxon hill forts, Pictish Brochs, or Viking place names, these signposts to the past tell not of one people but of many, all of them fighting to survive in an often inhospitable landscape.

THE SCOTTIE

Scotland is named after, and peopled by "the Scots"—the descendants of a number of different peoples long since conquered or assimilated. Looking back, the Scots' history and character seem etched in stone, but their ascendancy is far from certain. Scotland could have been called Pictland, Bretonland, Thorland, or even England.

The Gaelic-speaking Scot, or "Scottie," actually originated in Ireland. Around 500 B.C. they sailed across the Irish Sea and settled on the west coast of Scotland, mainly around Kinross, Oban, and the Isle of Jura. From there they spread along the west coast, introducing an early form of Christianity along the way. By the 9th century their king Kenneth MacAlpine had merged the Pictish and Scottish kingdoms into one, through conquest and marriage, and called it "Scotia."

It is an amazing feat that the kingdom of Scotia actually survived the dark early Middle Ages. They were constantly under threat by Vikings raiding along the coast from their northern base in Orkney, as well as the Roman-Britons and the Anglos in the South. To the North, the

Highlands remained impenetrable, filled with hostile and warring tribes. Internally, the kings were at loggerheads with feuding and ambitious noblemen.

Macbeth, Shakespeare's tale of murder and deceit, captures very well what must have been the mood of a time characterised by feuding, outright warfare, and dynastic struggle. Such is the superstition that surrounds Macbeth that in theatres it is only referred to as "that Scottish play," to avoid calling up its three witches with their boiling cauldron of bad luck.

The tale itself is based on real events. There was a Macbeth who ruled Scotia for 17 years after murdering the king, Duncan in 1040. Macbeth was himself killed by Duncan's son, Malcolm Canmore, in 1057 at Lumphanan near Aberdeen. Birnam Wood still stands outside Dunkeld. This is the same wood mentioned in Shakespeare's legend, which foretold of Macbeth's death by "coming to Dunsinane."

The lives of the early Scottish kings tended to be brutal and short and, most off them died with their boots on. But despite the kingdom's bloody ride through history, it did manage to survive, and by the 12th century had some semblance of unity and order. References to a Scottish Parliament, with a body of recognised law and a system of judicial officers, called *Judex,* dates back to the 12th century.

The Scots themselves didn't evolve from one ethnic group but from an enriched mixture of Scottie, Pict, Norman, and Roman Briton with a dash of Viking blood. Looking at the Scottish people today, with their mix of dark-haired to blond to striking redhead looks, is evidence enough of this fascinating intermingling of peoples and destinies.

So the truth is that they are, and have always been, many different voices, and their ancestors were as often as not cutting each other's throats during the nation's tumultuous formation. But if the birth of Scotland had little to do with ethnic consistency or political stability, where does the Scots' sense of themselves as a single people come from?

THE AULD ENEMY

Scotland's long-standing opposition and resistance to the "auld enemy"—the English—helped the country forge a clearer sense of itself as a distinct and independent nation. Ever since the first incursions by the Normans in the 12th century, the Scots have had to defend themselves from a numerically and economically stronger southern neighbour.

The Scottish peoples' resentment of their English neighbour is still palpable. There are certain pubs in the rougher areas of Edinburgh or Glasgow where it's best not to enter if you have an English accent. Every football or rugby match between England and Scotland is fiercely anticipated. Each victory by the Scots over the English on the playing field is like an act of revenge. Most Scots would rather support France or Germany when these countries play against England, instead of supporting the English.

This intense competitiveness and sense of common grievance has deep historical roots. As the historian George Mackay put it so succinctly, "No doubt it was in the logic of History that England would endeavour to absorb Scotland." The story of the Scots' early struggle to maintain their independence is an important one, as it set the pattern of Scottish resistance to English aggression that has echoed down the centuries.

The English king Edward I started the feud between the two nations after Scotland fell into civil war at the end of the 13th century. The Scottish king Alexander III died after a riding accident in 1286, leaving three rival claimants vying for the throne. Edward's attempts to "unite" Scotland and England, first through marriage and then by brute force, drove such a deep thorn into Scottish-English relations that it was to pitch the two nations into intermittent bloody warfare for the next three centuries.

Edward set up a nominal government north of the border under his control, enforced by an army that occupied most of the castles in the Scottish Lowlands. He even snatched the ultimate symbol of the Scots' political independence, the Stone of Destiny on which Scottish kings were traditionally invested, in Scone near Stirling. That the Stone of Destiny remained in Westminster for a further seven centuries, not to be returned to the Scots until 1996, is a good measure of England's desire for political hegemony over the whole island.

In the end, Edward and his son Edward II had bitten off more than they could chew. Led first by William Wallace and then Robert the Bruce, the Scots made an alliance with the French and rebelled. The country was plunged into a full-scale war of independence. For thirty years after 1285 the country's fate hung in the balance with the fortunes of both sides shifting between defeat and victory. The death of Edward I (known as the "Hammer of the Scots") in 1307, combined with Robert the Bruce's relentless guerrilla warfare from the Highlands, decided matters in favour of Scotland.

Robert the Bruce defeated an English army of up to 100,000 soldiers at the battle of Bannockburn in 1314. This resounding victory, one of the few decisive moments in Scottish history, paved the way for the formal recognition of Scottish independence at the treaty of Northampton in 1328.

Of course this wasn't the end. Rather, it set a pattern of English ambition and aggression in Scotland, countered by Scottish attempts to hold them off, even turning to France to even up the odds. The English and Scots continued to raid and kill each other across the borderland of the Southern Lowlands for centuries. The term "bereaved" comes from the Selkirk Reivers who were infamous for their bloody sorties into northern England. If you were "reived" you were certain to be bereaved. This area still has the desolate feel of a no man's land, a buffer zone between two hostile people whose history and land is stained with spilt blood.

Scotland did finally end up in a union with England, first through inheritance, when the Scottish King James VI inherited the English throne after the death of Queen Elizabeth in 1603, becoming James I of England. In 1707, under Anne of Orange, the Union of the Crown made the two countries effectively one. Scotland has since enjoyed more than two centuries of prosperous and peaceable alliance with England. Still, the memory of past grievances and of the full independence won by Robert the Bruce at Bannockburn hasn't faded. Political devolution from the Parliament in Westminster in 1999 and the strength of the Scottish Nationalist Party, now the main opposition party in the new parliament, is evidence enough of this.

RULE BRITANNIA

Although it's tempting to portray Scotland as one of history's underdogs, this is far from the truth. Scotland is still a part of Great Britain and has been for three centuries now. For the most part, that time has been successful, with the two "rivals" benefiting immensely from economic and political inter-dependence.

Political union with England in 1707 brought new opportunities for Scotland, as the Scots themselves were very quick to realise. The 18th and 19th centuries were a time of smug progress for the Scottish Lowlands as industrialisation and trade made the country increasingly affluent and self-confident.

Entrepreneurial in spirit and quick to seize upon new technological advances, the cities became centres for the production of linen, cotton, wool, paper, coal, and iron. From Edinburgh and Glasgow merchants traded these raw materials for luxuries such as tobacco, tea, and opium from countries as far flung as Egypt, North America, India, and Turkey. Many grew incredibly rich in the process.

The affluence of the 19th century can be seen in Edinburgh's New Town, with its towering streets of grey stone Georgian and Victorian houses, complete with Doric pillar entrances and sweeping cast iron staircases. Glasgow boasts the famous architect Charles Rennie Macintosh's visual feasts such as the Art College, which puts to shame the cheerless concrete shoeboxes many 20th century buildings resemble.

Such was Edinburgh's feeling of self-importance during colonial times that the residents built a huge Roman-style acropolis in Carlton Hill to the west of Princes Street, and dubbed the capital "the Athens of the North!" Blackened by petrol fumes the monument has lost some of its colonial grandeur and is now a gay cruising area, as well as a seasonal focal point for pagan rituals ushering in the summer or winter.

The Scots themselves became great travellers. In service of the Empire, many were posted overseas—in particular to India and South Africa—as missionaries, soldiers, administrators, or explorers. The most famous of Scottish explorers, David Livingstone (1813–1873), mapped out large areas of Africa only to be eventually swallowed up by it.

Nowadays hoards of young people still take off with a backpack and a traveller's journal to map out their own journeys of self-discovery. They tramp around far-flung destinations such as Australia, the Far East, and the Americas, often living on a shoestring and following the maxim that the greater the hardship and adventure, the more authentic the experience.

Many of these travellers are following in the footsteps of their forefathers and mothers. In the 19th century many without a viable future in Scotland left and travelled to the ends of the earth in search of frontiers where land and opportunity could be found. Rural poverty in the Highlands, and the landlords' zeal to introduce sheep into their lands, forced many abroad. New colonies established in North America, Australia, and New Zealand benefited immensely from these hardy and tenacious settlers. The place-names in these distant lands bear witness to how homesick the settlers were, often naming them after the places they had left behind. For example there are places named Glenelg in every one of these countries.

I remember reaching the last farm on the mainland of Southern Patagonia in Argentina to be greeted by a tall red-headed man in cowboy chaps and a chequered shirt. He told me in impeccable English how his great grandfather had travelled to Argentina from Scotland in the 1860s, marked out the land he needed, built a house and started rearing sheep. The original house still stands and little has changed since. His extended family exports wool across the globe and still maintains strong links with the old country in both language and customs.

The huge numbers of Scottish people who fled their homeland over the past two centuries go a long way towards explaining the peculiar nostalgic romance that Scotland holds in the hearts of so many. The land itself is dramatic and beautiful. The fact that so many Scots went unwillingly has made them regret leaving Scotland even more. Perhaps all that homesick dreaming has conjured up an imagined Scotland. No wonder there are so many companies offering to trace genealogies for distant clan relatives.

Empire Ups and Downs

As Scotland took to the seas it became an international centre for shipbuilding. From the 1840s Aberdeen was building the tall sailing ships, or clippers, that chased the tradewinds around the world, competing with America in the Chinese opium trade. With the invention of steam engines and iron-hulled boats, the Clyde River in Glasgow, and to a lesser extent Leith docks in Edinburgh, became the centres of the Scottish shipping industry. In 1870 the Clyde docks employed 20,000 men and Scotland produced 70 % of the iron-hulled ships launched in Britain.

The Age of Empire brought with it the era of "Scottish Enlightenment," a time of great advances in science and the arts. To mention a few famous names, there was James Watt, inventor of a more efficient steam engine, and Alexander Bell who devised the first telephone. There were also several famous thinkers, notably the geographer James Hutton, philosopher David Hume, and economist Adam Smith.

By the end of the 18th century, Scottish doctors had made such a reputation for themselves that they were in demand across Europe. The Russian Tsars, Peter the Great, and Alexander I, as well as Catherine II, all had Scottish physicians. Most famed of them all was Sir James Young Simpson, who discovered chloroform. Such was the general flowering of the time that Voltaire once quipped, "At the present time it is from Scotland we receive rules of taste in all the arts."

As much as this period of British history glitters for Scotland it did not come without cost. The philosophy of economic laissez faire, in which the individual pursuit of maximum economic reward was expected to somehow benefit all, ended up benefiting the few. In the 18th century, Scotland became an increasingly urban society as thousands abandoned their fields in search of work in the big industries in the South. City life often brought untold misery to the thousands who came in search of that ever elusive better life.

Cripplingly low wages at the looms, pits, and shipyards made Scottish industries profitable but left a lasting legacy of urban deprivation. With an inadequate diet and cramped living conditions—whole families often shared a single room—diseases such as smallpox, consumption, fever, and "bowel hives" took a terrible toll. Infant mortality rates during this period speak for themselves. An examination of 1,508 deaths in the city parish of Glasgow in 1791 revealed that 694 of those were under the age of two. Until 1850, half of all those who died in Glasgow were under the age of 10!

The old town in Edinburgh was so disease-infested that much of it was finally sealed off and eventually rebuilt. However, the smart new Georgian buildings, called the New Town, were no less forgiving to the city's underprivileged. The grand steps that run up to the front entrance disguise the basements from which the landed, professional, and merchant classes were served. A whole army of scullerymaids, kitchenmaids, parlourmaids, tablemaids, lady's maids, housekeepers, cooks, footmen, valets, and butlers served and lived under their masters in the main house.

These divisions, despite a large and affluent middle class, are still evident in the enormous gap between rich and poor, with low wages barely sustaining large sectors of the economy. In recent years, for example, a proliferation of call centres for businesses and services have sprung up, made profitable by low wages, long hours, and very limited union protection. The fact that low-income people are still crammed into council estates on the outskirts of towns is rarely commented on. The 19th century system of exploitation—justified by those great Victorian landmarks of "progress," empire and industrialisation—has made such levels of poverty an accepted part of reality to this day.

Scotland's participation as part of Great Britain and the Empire went largely unquestioned throughout the 19th century and survived two world wars. This shared history brought with it a common identity and being British still holds considerable currency amongst older generations of Scots. Many Scots who remember World War II and the hard years of rationing afterwards have a clear sense of nationality, considering themselves first to be British and only secondly Scottish.

This has as much to do with World Wars I and II as with the memory of empire. The Scots, Welsh, Irish, and English stood and fought as one in both wars. They shed the same blood and still rub shoulders, albeit in graves and memorials. Their sacrifice in the defence of Great Britain is a shared one.

Mind you, that doesn't mean you can confuse a Scot with an Englishman without getting a few sharp words in reply. Much like the Canadians' prickly relations with their neighbours to the south, it's best not to jump in and say, "So you're from England" when you meet someone from the Gilded Isle until you're sure they are truly "English." However for someone from the British Isles to say that they're from Britain, rather than Northern Ireland, England, Scotland, or Wales, is still common.

In many ways it's a noble sentiment. Feeling part of a union of differing nations, whether it is Great Britain, the former Yugoslavia or Europe, allows for greater cooperation and dampens the ugly side of nationalism: xenophobia and racism.

However, that sentiment is fast fading amongst the younger generations. For Scots in their twenties and thirties, being British seems increasingly irrelevant these days. As Alistair Allen, parliamentary aid for the Scottish Nationalist Party told me, "People who don't have a recollection of Empire, or crucially the Second World War, really have very little notion of what Britishness is."

"D" IS FOR DEVOLUTION

I saw two Scotsmen standing still on George IV Bridge in Edinburgh one day staring across the road. The rain was coming down hard as they tried to make out the name, written in Gaelic and English, on the blue plaque on the building opposite. "I cannea believe it, it's the parliament" said one with a giggle. His friend was speechless, it just wouldn't sink in.

There is still an air of disbelief for many about the new Scottish Parliament. After all it's been almost three hundred years coming and as recently as the early 1990s Scottish political devolution from England still seemed as likely as the Scots winning the World Cup.

In June 1999 the new Parliament was officially opened by the Queen with much pomp, marking an exciting new chapter for a more confident and independent nation. Scotland certainly has come a long way since its ambitions were so interlinked with the fate of the British Empire. The story of Scotland in the 20th century is one of the Scots' growing realisation that they need and want a greater say in their own future and their success in making this a reality at last.

The British Empire is now honoured with little more than a few museums in London bulging with explorers' loot. In fact, the wind-swept Falkland Islands in the South Pacific are now nearly the last tangible reminder of Britain's colonial past. Others, such as today's India and Pakistan, have long since become independent states.

It's now hard to imagine that at the end of the 19th century, British control and influence spread across a third of the world's landmass. Britain's self-confidence, her superiority, and the march of her progress seemed assured. Scotland's part in this went unquestioned, that is, until the economic bubble burst north of the border.

By the beginning of the 20th century the glories of empire had started to lose their sheen for Scotland. Competition from countries with even cheaper labour costs helped make the big labour intensive industries such as iron and cotton increasingly unproductive. But rising unemployment is only part of the story.

World War I decimated a generation of men and punctured the confidence that so many had held in the logic of Empire and the inevitability of progress. Europe had proved itself to be as much a centre for barbarism as a centre for the spread of "civilisation" to dependant states. By the 1930s, unemployment exceeded 20% in Scotland and Soviet Bolshevism was on the march in Clydeside.

World War II brought a brief Indian summer on the economic front, with a revival in demand for the big ships of trade and war, bringing money to the docks and yards of Aberdeen, Glasgow, and Edinburgh. But the writing was on the wall—Scotland increasingly became a poor hinterland to the financial and consumer boom in the southeast of England. With the axing of many rail lines and bus routes in Scotland after the Beeching Report in 1963, the country's disappearance into a northern isolation seemed complete.

With Scotland's economy controlled from Westminster and practically no political say on the domestic or international stage, the country might have seemed to have quietly slipped off the world map. The North of England, synonymous to most southerners with darkness, poverty and deprivation, could have extended all the way to John O'Groats, and Scotland the nation could have been left to the memory of history books and old wives' tales.

But in the end there was too much to Scotland, it was too distinct and proud to give up so easily. As well as the Scots' strong sense of themselves as being culturally distinct from the English, the original 1707 Act of Union with England allowed Scotland to keep its own practices in law and education, which it has done ever since. Scotland has clung to its sense of individual and separate identity with continued tenacity.

The Scottish National Party first found a real voice in Scottish hearts from the late 1960s with its calls for independence. The discovery of oil, dubbed "black gold" by locals, 177 km (110 miles) off the coast of Aberdeen in October 1970 suddenly made the idea of political independence an economic reality for the Scots. It was just a matter of time before the old drums of resistance to rule from the south started beating again.

For the two main parties in Britain—the Conservatives and Labour—full independence has always been out of the question. However the idea of some level of regional devolution for Scotland and Wales has been batted about since the early 1970s. In 1979 the Labour Party took the country to the brink with a referendum for devolution. Although 51.6 % voted "yes," it was deemed inconclusive. It would be Scotland's last chance to have a say on the matter for another eighteen years.

Ask the Scots what made it obvious to them that they needed their own Parliament again and they'll most likely reply, "Margaret Thatcher." Although the "iron lady" kept up her support in England throughout the 1980s, the Scots never had much time for her. In 1988, the height of her political fortunes in England, Scottish football supporters showed her a sea of red cards and practically whistled her out of the national stadium at Hampden Park when she made a rare visit north of the border. They spoke as a nation increasingly beleaguered by rising unemployment and neglect from Westminster.

Thatcher's commitment to open market economics did not protect Scotland's ailing industries. The textile, shipping, and coal industries collapsed as Scotland shed a third of its jobs between 1979 and 1981. The Conservatives showed little interest in Scotland, confident their popularity in the south would outweigh poor showings in Scotland.

Soaring unemployment in the 1980s and 1990s brought a new face to Scotland: desperation, drug abuse, and a prevailing sense of hopelessness. This is the Scotland of the film *Trainspotting* where directionless youths stumble from one heroin fix to another and then into crime to pay for their habit.

Although the scale of drug abuse has declined since the early 1990s (Edinburgh was Europe's heroin capital until AIDS killed many of its addicts), Scotland still has the habit for substance abuse picked up in the last couple of generations. The number of homeless people on the streets is a lasting testimony to just how many have lost their way in the past 20 years.

When Scotland finally had another say over the question of devolution after a landslide victory by the "new" Labour Party in 1997, they didn't falter. In the referendum held on the September 11, 1997, an overwhelming majority of (74.3%) of the nation voted for devolution and 63.5% voted for tax-raising powers. Scotland had gone full circle, building a new and daringly modern parliament opposite the site of the old one in Holyrood Palace.

The Scottish Parliament

The change to Scotland's political landscape has been much further reaching than a flash-looking Parliament building, due to be completed in 2004 at considerable public expense. Scotland's first political representatives, or members of the Scottish parliament (MSPs), were first elected in 1999 in a system of proportional representation. This is a big divergence from traditional British politics where the party that gets the most votes in national elections, wins office. The "first past the post" policy often ends in a predictable confrontation between the two big hitters, Labour and Conservative, with little real say from the smaller parties on the fringes.

In contrast, Proportional Representation in Scotland hopes to encourage a more consensual style of politics. Proportional Representation is an electoral system in which each political party is represented in a government according to its actual voting strength in the electorate. Win 60% of the vote and you get 60% of the seats. This forces parties to work together to find common ground and ensures that smaller parties and interest groups have a say in the decision-making process. That there are MSPs in the Scots parliament representing the Green party and the Scottish Socialist party is in some measure, a new and more inclusive style of politics for the 21st century.

However, the new Parliament has found it hard to live up to the very high expectations placed upon it. While successfully legislating on issues such as education and land reform, the Scottish Executive has also suffered its share of scandal and criticism from the press.

The First Minister Henry McLeish had to step down in 2002 over revelations of murky financial dealings. Promised reforms, such as land reform, have been losing momentum and there is growing unease over the soaring price tag of the new parliament building. Henry McLeish's successor, Jack McConnell, has managed to keep the ship afloat but there is still much to prove.

Although the jury is still out on the Scottish Parliament's overall success, the idea remains a sound one. With Wales and Northern Ireland also experimenting with devolution, this could be the beginning of a new federal system of representation in Britain, rather than power remaining centred in London.

"I" IS FOR INDEPENDENCE

For many, and in particular the Scottish Nationalist Party, devolution is not enough. The argument goes that if Scotland is to truly grasp its own destiny, nothing less than full independence is enough. This logic holds some weight; Parliament in Westminster still reserves judgement over big matters such as macroeconomics, foreign policy, defence, social security, and broadcasting. The Scottish Parliament's survival is still dependent on Westminster, the British State can still dissolve Scotland's fragile federalism any time it wishes.

Moreover, Scotland's say in the council of ministers in Europe is still very limited compared to other even smaller independent states such as Denmark or Luxembourg. To avoid slipping back into the parochialism and isolation of the 1970s, nationalists claim that Scotland needs a full say amongst the member states of the European Union and NATO. The old debate continues...

In the meantime, many Scots are asking questions about themselves. With that auld enemy England no longer looming over the border, there is a new questioning of old political and religious orthodoxy and a new interest in redefining the undefinable—what is Scotland?

For some the answer is in the past, not so much in what Scotland is but in what it was and how the old ways can be revived to meet the modern world. Others want to drop the "tartan and shortbread" image and forge a new, modern identity. The Arts Council, a government body, has criticised Scotland's traditional image as being too quaint and stuffy. It wants to seek out a new emphasis on "plurality and diversity, tradition and contemporary innovation." A drop in tourism to the country in recent years perhaps shows that the old formulas are starting to wear a little thin.

Many look across the seas to Europe for inspiration and a more rooted sense of place. It's strange considering that the British Isles has fostered an image of separation from the rest of Europe in the past. After all, the British love to be different. They drive on the left rather than the right, have given up an imperial system of measurement and still prefer warm flat beer to cold and fizzy lager! Disquiet over integration into the European Union stems from an islander's sense that Europe is best kept "over there" beyond the fog and icy waters of the English Channel.

The old clichés about Britain's blissful island isolation don't ring as true for the Scots as it does for the English. Whether invaded by the Vikings, allied with France, or as part of a colonial empire, there has always been close contact between the Scots and other European peoples. Scotland's political and cultural aspirations are aimed as much towards the European Community as towards England. Perhaps these northern souls will come to consider themselves as Scots first and Europeans second, dropping the British identity altogether.

In the end, the very idea of a single Scottish people or identity is as much of a myth as the tourist images of the ginger-haired Highlander or the Loch Ness monster. The people and landscape are just too diverse to sit easily under one banner and who would want to daub a country with the same dull cultural wash anyway? As archaeologist Mairi Black bluntly put it: "The only thing that the Scots have in common is heart disease."

A bit of soul searching brought about by a new Parliament isn't necessarily a bad thing. The essential nature of Scotland may defy a simple definition but the curiosity, the questions asked, and the road of discovery itself may be enough.

"Rebirth, renewal, renaissance" is scrawled in deep Prussian blue on a little old hut on Govan pier, overlooked by some of the worst housing estates in Leith. It's yet to come to Scotland but the desire and the will for new vision and purpose is stronger now than it's been for a very long while.

FLAGS AND ANTHEMS

The flag of Scotland—a white diagonal cross on a blue field—is called a Saltire. It symbolises St Andrew, the patron saint of Scotland.

The Saltire was first said to have appeared in the sky to the Pictish King Hungus before he trounced the Anglo-Saxons at the battle of Aethelstaneford. It has been used as a symbol for the struggle of independence since the middle of the 14th century.

The national flag of the United Kingdom—the Union Jack— also flies in Scotland. The flag combines the cross of St George, the patron saint of England with the cross of St Andrews and a cross similar to Ireland's patron, St Patrick.

The official national anthem throughout the UK remains *God Save the Queen*. However the Scottish have adopted *Flower of Scotland*, *Scotland the Brave*, and William Jackson's *Land of Light* as their own anthems. Another sentimental favourite is Robert Burns' *Auld Lang Syne*, traditionally sung over New Year Hogmanay celebrations. At sporting events, especially rugby internationals, Scottish fans fly the blue and white Saltire flag and sing *Flower of Scotland*.

— Chapter Two —

NORTHERN EXPOSURE

"As Dr Johnson never said, 'Is there any Scotsman
without charm?'"

—Sir J.M. Barrie, British novelist, author and play-
wright, in an address to Edinburgh University

Trying to tease a "national character" out of the Scots is not easy. For
every supposed character trait there are a thousand exceptions and
many of the stereotypes are far from consistent. The Scots are
portrayed as being openhearted and generous, courageous, tightfisted
and dour, high-spirited and cynical—all at the same time. Drawing a
clear thread through all these supposed traits and characteristics is
impossible. The best course of action is to take all generalisations with
a healthy pinch of salt.

Part of the difficulty lies in presuming the Scots to be one people, one unified "type." The Scots are just as clearly marked by their differences as their similarities.

They come together to pour scorn on the English, or celebrate a national sporting victory, but they are also divided by class, geography and prejudice—some as deep as the fault lines that divide the country itself. So any Northern Exposure can only be skin deep—a cursory look at some of the similarities and contradictions that make up the Scottish people, bonded as they are by the same history, language, and salty land.

POPULAR SCOTTISH STEREOTYPES

Open and Friendly Folk

Watch an old black-and-white war film and you will invariably see English, Welsh, and Scots soldiers bunkered up together on a front line, united in their animosity toward the Germans. The Scot, often called Jimmy, bubbles with chatty exuberance. His English and Welsh companions are usually more circumspect, displaying a stoic reserve under fire.

This is a classic image of the Scot, upbeat and full of easy banter. It is also pretty accurate. Most travellers who visit Scotland comment on how friendly the people are. Whether buying something in a shop or just waiting for a bus, it's easy to slip into conversation with locals. Scots love to chat, and will pass comment on pretty much anything. They are a friendly and approachable people and nowhere is this more evident than in Glasgow.

Wander around Glasgow and you would think you were in a small village rather than a big city—so many people have the time to stop and exchange a few friendly words. This is a marked difference from southern England where reserve and tact rule the day. The trend in Britain is that the further north you go, the warmer the people tend do be, in inverse relation to the climate.

To Be Tight

That said, the picture of the Scots isn't all rosy. On the other side of the coin they are often characterised for being careful or even tightfisted with their money. It is certainly a common perception held abroad. In Greece locals often say "stop being Scottish," if someone is reluctant to part with their money.

England is awash with jokes about the Scots' legendary frugality, most of them as tired and hackneyed as the jibes about the Irish being stupid (which also couldn't be further from the truth). One of the few half-decent jokes is of an Englishman and a Scotsman in a pub together. The Englishman spots a fly in his beer and, complaining bitterly, demands a new pint from the barman. The Scotsman likewise sees a fly in his drink, gingerly picks it out of the froth and holding it in front of his face by the legs hisses, "Spit it out you wee bastard."

The Scots themselves are happy to have a laugh at their famed meanness with money, although Aberdeen usually seems to come out worst. A common joke in Glasgow is that if you knock on someone's door at teatime (dinner) in Glasgow, the host will invite you in saying, "Come in and have your tea." If you do the same in Edinburgh they'll say, "Oh, you'll have had your tea." In Aberdeen you'll be presented a wonderful spread of food and drink, laid out on the dining room table—with a price tag neatly attached to everything.

The image of the Scots being tight may be a source of mirth on both sides of the border but it's best not to take these jokes too seriously. With Scotland having been a poor relation to much of Western Europe for centuries, its people are accustomed to being prudent with money. I know two Scots brothers who are so conscientious of their expenditure that it looks like they are pulling teeth rather than pound coins every time they open their skinny wallets.

However when it comes to hospitality, to friends or strangers alike, money doesn't enter the equation. The Scots are equally famed for their open-hearted generosity. Get invited over for a meal and every effort is made to prepare a generous spread. It's almost rude not to accept second helpings. Likewise in a bar, if you get chatting to a stranger they will include you in a round of drinks, even if they're down to their last pennies.

Spirited Warriors

Scotland is a small nation with a big heart, or so the story goes. The image of the Scots beating back their brutish English neighbour is an enduring one. It has generated an imagined landscape of Scotland the brave, a united warlike people fighting off a far greater foe.

Such is the romance of this image that there is a whole society called Clan Wallace that carry on the clansmen's cause. They dress up in tartan, wearing T-shirts with slogans like "Kill more with a claymore," and ride around hanging tough on motorbikes. Together they supply the demand for wild and hairy Scotsmen in films such as *Ivanhoe* and *Braveheart*. But the Scots' tenacious spirit isn't just re-enacted in films. At international sporting events, especially rugby, the Scots genuinely come together to cheer their nation on in a single voice. Players and fans put in 110% commitment, whoever the opponent and whatever the odds are against them.

There is nothing to match the atmosphere in Murrayfield Stadium in Edinburgh at a "six nations" rugby match when the Scots urge their team to yet another Herculean effort. It was like that in April 2000 when Scotland wrestled a grand slam victory from England and broke a ten-year losing streak against their greatest of opponents.

Facing an English team buoyant after beating France, Ireland, and Italy, only the weather added an element of chance to what seemed a foregone conclusion. The rain came down in torrents, and seemed to sweep the players and the whole pitch into a grey oblivion. The rain switched to hail and some 60,000 Scots sung on their team in the wintry downpour. In the end Scotland won 19–13 and whether or not you like rugby, you simply had to admire their victory. Through sheer strength-of-spirit the Scottish team had outplayed a stronger opponent.

That the Scots are a proud and nationalistic people is beyond doubt. Whether sporting performances such as these draw on a national tendency of fierce warlike resilience in the face of adversity is another question.

American immigrant Pearson Fernside who has lived in Scotland for five years seems to think so. He explained "The Scots are a decent, hardy and tenacious people who tend to drink too much."

The Hard Man

The image of Scotland as a nation of spirited warriors is a little one-sided. After all it's hard to be one of those sporran-swinging clansmen, or rugby players battling on the field if you're a woman. Scotland is something of a macho society, where the hard man still cuts a provocative swagger across the nation's collective psyche.

Try and imagine prominent Scottish women who stand out as emblematic symbols of Scottish history or contemporary culture. Flora MacDonald and Mary Queen of Scots jump immediately to mind, after that it all gets a bit thin on the ground.

In contrast there are a whole host of Scotsmen famed for one enduring feat or another: James VI of Scotland for becoming King of England, David Livingstone for finding Victoria Falls before getting lost, Sean Connery for being Sean Connery... the list is endless.

It isn't just that men have got the lion's share of the press in Scotland. The famous ones are usually loveable rogues—macho, gritty and never too far from a fight. Some of the first Scottish "big men" to make names for themselves were, oddly enough, saints. Around the 6th century, the legend of St Columba who came to Scotland from Ireland to convert the pagans to Christianity, is far from being a story of a peaceful monk. He is said to have taken to the woods to single-handedly slay wolves and wild boars to prove his manhood.

Scottish male heroes have been living and dying by the sword ever since the beginning of history, and probably before. Just watch a James Bond film with Sean Connery and see the 20th century idol of many Scots—a dashing and ruthless womaniser with nothing to loose. Robert Carlyle's terrifying "Begsby" from the movie *Trainspotting* also plays out a more contemporary version of this rough and uncompromising spirit. Characters like Begsby also point to a dark underbelly of frustration and violence in Scotland, tucked away from prying eyes by the best work of the Scottish Tourist Board.

A Good Laugh

The Scots are known abroad for their sense of humour. This is hardly surprising given that one of their greatest ambassadors overseas, Billy Connolly, is a comedian. Billy Connolly—or the Big Yin as they call him in his hometown of Glasgow—now lives and works in America. But his humour remains an enduring example of Scottish wit at its sharpest—fast, irreverent, and self-deprecating.

Billy Connolly comes from a long line of Scottish jokers to hit the stage or television screens in the last century. They date back to the old music hall comedians such as Stanley Baxter and Sir Harry Lauder. They played drunken hard men even when sober, men with sharp tongues and sentimental hearts. Glasgow was always a great one for pantomimes; the sound of the boos and hisses of the audiences would carry for streets around the theatres that they were held in.

Some of the best comedy still comes out of Glasgow, most notably the television series *Rab C. Nesbitt* and *Chewin' the Fat*. The humour in Ian Patterson's screenplay character Rab C. Nesbitt borders on self-hate; the ramblings of a beer-touting working-class guy whose stream of broad Scots speech needed subtitles to be understood properly in England. He represents a grimmer reality to Glasgow, where poverty and desperation (as well as humour) is a part of many people's lives. Rab is the reeling, swearing contradiction to the Glasgow of boutiques and European coffee shops that just will not go away.

Humour is not reserved for the professional comedians in Scotland. Pretty much anyone can hold an audience, tell a great story, and get a good laugh at the end of it. In most areas of Scotland a fast wit is revered. At school you can be a stunted child with specs and still command the respect of the big lads if you can cut them down with a few quick words (and survive the beating).

There was one old boy on the west coast who lived in a caravan and made his living from telling jokes and stories to passing tourists. He would wander down to the local bar, groomed to perfection in a tweed suit, tie, and hat. There he would weave fantastic stories to appreciative tourists who would buy him drinks and food in return. And so he survived for many years, never, or so they say, telling the same story twice.

Dour

Bizarrely, Scots are considered to be dour—serious, cynical and downbeat—as well as high-spirited and funny. The old black-and-white version of the classic film *The Thirty-Nine Steps* has a typical portrayal of the dour Scotsman. The dashing young hero takes refuge in an old farmhouse in the Highlands whilst fleeing from the police. The farmer is a long-faced cantankerous old character that lives a meagre existence of hard work and self-discipline. His wife however is young, beautiful, and lonely; I needn't tell you the rest.

This image may not do the Scots any favours but it does have a historical basis. While the English took on the Protestant Reformation in the 16th century halfheartedly, in Scotland, Calvinism swept the country and the Church, or Kirk, took a keen interest in all aspects of social custom. Pleasures such as dancing, singing, and sex outside of marriage were effectively banned in place of a life of simple austerity and hard, honest work.

Although the days of supremacy of the Kirk are long over in all but the most isolated communities, the stereotype of the dour Scotsman or woman is a hangover from those times. Older "God-fearing" Scots can still have a certain severity to them. One friend's father, who is a retired minister used to ask him every evening when he was a boy, "Well son, what have you done today to justify your existence?"

AN ISLAND PEOPLE

Perhaps the one quality that draws these people and all their contradictions together is the sea. It is easy to lose sight of the fact that Britain is a big island. Live in central Scotland, dominated by inland lakes and mountains, and you may very rarely make it to the coast. But at no point in Great Britain are you more than 121 km (75 miles) from the sea. All roads eventually lead to the ocean and the sense of being cut off makes for a distinctive people.

The people on the coasts and small isles around Scotland, on those fringes where water and land meet, exemplify this spirit. With a fierce sense of themselves they can be independent and stubborn in their ways. They can also be friendly and high-spirited. With that independent streak comes the love of a good "crack," making for lively and fun conversations. Pop into a small store, a bar or a post office and you'll find yourself chatting away about anything from the time of day to upcoming elections.

With the softness of the milder west coast climate, a complete stranger will walk up with that sunbeam of a greeting, "'Tis a grand day." I remember an old boy stopping me to talk about the horses and how his bets had been faring for a good half-hour before disappearing with a parting "cheerio."

But an island people can also hold a lot back. A cool northern climate, salty air and a sense of isolation breeds caution. Meet someone by chance and they will be friendly. Getting close to them in small communities can be another story altogether.

People surrounded by the sea can also be cagey and secretive, and this is not surprising, given their harsh lives. Fishing communities around Scotland have borne the brunt of the Irish and North Seas for centuries and boats are still occasionally lost. Although the lifeboat stations that dot the coast frequently save lives, someone in the water this far north has little chance of surviving the cold. Such a tough and lonely existence brings an immense respect for the sea and with it, circumspection on land.

Perhaps a certain secretiveness also draws on deeper historical roots. Celtic people have always had to protect their cultural and political independence, whether in Cornwall, Scotland, Wales or Ireland. After the Battle of Culloden, (see chapter nine) an army of occupation was stationed in barracks outside of Highland settlements, repressing ancient practices such as the speaking of Gaelic. Language and tradition had to be remembered and passed on in secret.

The smaller coastal communities also held secrets of a more commercial nature. There is a long tradition of smuggling in Scotland. For centuries communities up and down the coast have seen small boats of contraband in the dead of night. Smugglers spun many folk tales of devils and ghostly beings in caves to keep people away at night. For example the Smoo cave in Durness on the north coast is said to be a portal to hell, but has also been a favoured portal for tax-free goods.

The Mock Scot

So where does this leave the traditional images of the Scot, all those bonnie lasses and gallant ginger-haired lads in kilts? They still live on in the heads of those who wish to believe Sir Walter Scott's romances. Enter the mock Scot, who usually lives outside Scotland but claims some obscure link with the "old country."

There is no shortage of distant relatives to Scotland that hold a genuine claim. An estimated 20 million Scottish descendants are scattered across the world, around four times as many as live in Scotland itself.

The mock Scot lives for Burns Night, tartan, and country dancing. I remember one night coming across a Scottish dancing group in Bolivia of all places. The dancers turned out to be English, claiming Scottishness through distant relatives. Perhaps they were too embarrassed by the dismal English equivalent to Scots reels—called Morris dancing—to claim it as their own. One girl had the audacity to claim, "I went to Edinburgh University, that makes me Scottish."

The saddest aspect of this image of Scotland, of sporrans and cock-a-leekie broth, is that it fixes the country firmly in a past that never really existed in the first place. Heather-tinted spectacles constantly blur Scotland's place in the new millennium. Romantic images of the Scotland of lochs and mountains are inevitable but the danger is that they will end up overshadowing Scotland today, a vibrant and forward-looking nation.

DIVIDED WE STAND

I stopped to chat with a homeless man on the street one day. He asked me if I was a student before ranting against all students, barely drawing breath between invectives. A man in a big car with a suit caught his eye and he moved on to rich people, saying they were all snobs and middle class bastards who only cared about their cheque books. Next came the English: "Soft southern losers the lot of them," he spat. I wanted to ask him if there was anyone he didn't hate, but thought better of it.

Everything is not as it seems in Scotland. Despite the country's popular image as a hospitable and peaceable nation, like anywhere else in the world there is plenty of room for hatred and prejudice. In defining the Scots it is just as important to look at their differences as well as their similarities.

Rich and Poor

Pass through Edinburgh and Glasgow and you can't help but be impressed. Edinburgh's city centre—Princess Gardens, the Castle and the Royal Mile—are breathtaking. Glasgow has less of the old stone facades but more of the frenetic big city vibe with its big glass buildings, art galleries, and boutiques. Visit some of the residential areas close to the centre and the picture is complete. Affluent areas such as Bearsden in Glasgow and Morningside in Edinburgh, with their smart cars and well-clipped gardens, point to a wealthy and contented society. Although the affluent middle class is real in Scotland, it's a mistake to think that this is the norm.

This is Scotland: poverty and decay in one of the worst housing estates in Glasgow.

In part it's a clever illusion; a thinly painted veneer of Georgian grandeur laid on for residents and visitors alike. Behind those impressive streets the cities have a darker story to tell, a story of poverty, drug abuse and neglect. Housed in decaying government-built "housing estates,"—either tenement flats or high-rise blocks—Scotland's urban poor have little in the way of work, education, or hope. Most of the estates they live in are tucked out of sight and out of mind.

Glasgow has the most visible problems, dating back to the days of the Industrial Revolution when thousands were crammed into single room tenement buildings to work in the factories and yards. In rougher areas in the east and north of the city—such as Easterhouse and Possil—the only substantive change nowadays is that most of the industry that once sustained these populations has dropped away, leaving a legacy of unemployment, desperation, and alcohol or drug abuse. There are thought to be upwards of 10,000 heroin users alone in Glasgow, the highest concentration in Britain.

The story is a similar one in cities and towns across Scotland. The poorer areas of Edinburgh are a long, long way from the grandeur of the New Town.

Ben, aged 19, who lives in the Wester Hales estate, said, "It's about survival. There's no proper heating in the flat and I live on the ninth floor, so I have to board up the windows every winter to stop the wind blowing them in."

Aberdeen is no exception, "boasting" one of the highest gaps between rich and poor in Great Britain. With no real political will to address these vast inequalities in Scottish society, the Scotland of Irvine Welsh's *Trainspotting* looks set to endure. As the Society of Gal-Gael, concerned with urban regeneration, puts it, "The culture of Scotland, so rich in Celtic, Pict, and Norse traditions, has been reduced to tourist clichés, whilst mass unemployment, inner city urban decay and social alienation have produced a culture of dependency, drug addiction and violence."

Many Scots live in gritty urban environments, making few trips into the countryside that makes their nation so famous. In the film *Trainspotting*, Renton and his pals take a break from their drug-frenzied lives in Edinburgh to go for a walk in the country. On arrival in the big outdoors they wonder around confused and disorientated before returning to the familiarity of their granite jungle.

There is also a broad gulf of experience between those who grow up in the country and those from the cities. Several community projects are working to bring these two worlds together. For example the Camas project set up by the Iona Community brings children from deprived and inner city backgrounds to some old fishing cottages on the island of Mull. There they spend up to two weeks walking along the coast, abseiling off cliffs, and gardening.

Camas' director Rachel McCann told me, "It's a real culture shock for the kids when they first come here, one boy didn't even know that chips come from potatoes. But by the end of their stay none of them want to leave."

Class System

The class system is one of Britain's trademarks, an unwritten social hierarchy that has been established over several centuries. Although it may not be so readily apparent to the outsider, most people in Scotland belong to a particular social class, however much they might prefer to deny it.

British society is roughly divided into three classes. The working classes are traditionally poorer, disadvantaged, and work in areas such as industry, skilled labour, and trades. The middle classes, who represent a wide range of people, are better educated, wealthier, and tend to take on professions such as medicine and law. The upper classes, aristocracy or "blue blood" as they are occasionally termed aren't always rich, but have millennias of privilege to keep them at the top of the heap.

This is only a thumbnail sketch and there are plenty of rebels, exceptions, and anomalies but it does give some idea of the broad divisions that exist in Scottish society. The clearest marker is schooling. Children who are sent to private schools (confusingly called public schools) tend to be from upper-middle class or upper class families. Children sent to state schools are more likely to be from lower-middle or lower classes. However it's also much more complex than that. The area you live in, your accent, dress sense, and even your diet, all serve to "class-ify" you.

Common to all class consciousness are varying degrees of misunderstanding and snobbery. Just as a labourer will sneer at someone with a public school accent, so the middle classes can look down on the working classes with a mix of disdain and fear. It's often easier to be a total outsider.

Lucy Grant, an American who has lived in both Scotland and England for over 25 years, swears that her status as a foreigner has been socially advantageous. Unable to place her, the British are forced to take her as she is rather than box her into a class and judge her by that.

Protestant and Catholic

On the west coast of Scotland and especially in and around Glasgow, there is a strong "sectarian divide" between Protestants and Catholics. Although nominally about religion, in reality this division runs much deeper than just which church people attend on a Sunday. It ties into history, identity and soccer. Sectarianism is so deeply embedded in some areas that, like the ongoing "troubles" in Northern Ireland, there seems little way out of an impasse that defies the logic of negotiation.

The confrontation between Catholics and Protestants dates back to the potato famine in Ireland in the 1840s. Unable to survive in Ireland, tens of thousands of poor Irish immigrants came to the west coast of Scotland in search of work. Such a large influx of Irish Catholics was quickly seen as a threat to the Protestant Scottish community. Before long whole communities in Glasgow were divided along national and religious lines. Today the distinction between Irish and Scottish has long since blurred but the memory of mutual resentment and religious intolerance has endured.

In Northern Ireland these sectarian divisions still rage on in the streets, but in Scotland they are largely confined to the football pitch. Football in Glasgow is much more than a spectator sport. It is an all-consuming passion that encompasses sport, religion, and ultimately politics. It is hardly surprising that Glasgow is the only city in Europe that houses three 50,000 plus capacity football stadiums—Ibrox, Celtic Park, and Hampden Park.

The two biggest football clubs in Scotland, Rangers and Celtic, mirror the sectarian divide. Rangers' fans come predominantly from the Protestant community and Celtic fans are mostly drawn from the Catholic community.

The two camps of supporters are incredibly loyal and devoted to their respective teams. Team colours, white and green for Celtic and blue for Rangers, are worn with swaggering pride. For many, a loss on the football pitch is taken as a personal blow; success is met with jubilation bordering on hysteria.

Both Celtic and Rangers clubs have non-sectarian policies but their supporters are under no illusions. Such is the animosity between the two sides that twenty years ago, pitched battles raged in the stands and even on the pitch itself. These days violence is usually limited to verbal abuse but the centre of Glasgow is still a virtual no-go area the night after a Rangers-Celtic match. Many of the pubs bar anyone wearing team colours to avoid trouble. For soccer fans who want no part of this collective insanity, there is always Partick Thistle, whose Protestant and Catholic patrons stay clear of the sectarian divide.

This ancient confrontation between Catholics and Protestants peaks in and around Glasgow with the Orange March on July 12. This is when members of the Protestant "Orange Order" march through the streets to symbolically assert their authority over the Catholic community. There is seldom any violence but as the procession marches through Catholic areas you can cut the atmosphere with a knife.

The march, repeated across Northern Ireland, reasserts a cycle of resentment and violence that seems inexhaustible. A friend told me once how he saw grown men on an Orange march in Lanark hurl verbal abuse at a passing child of six or seven just because he was wearing a Celtic football top.

Highlanders vs Lowlanders

Geography has always divided Scotland and its inhabitants. The Lowlands, that broad swath of agricultural land that makes up Southern Scotland, supports the bulk of the population. Better connected by land and sea, the Lowlands have been the centre of the industrial revolution, cultural expression and political representation in Scotland for centuries.

In contrast the Highlands have remained on the margin, stubbornly independent and considered for centuries a savage backwater (see chapter 10). Fear and loathing has traditionally cut both ways. In the past, Highlanders have been quick to write off Lowlanders as soft anglophiles who had lost touch with their Celtic roots. The old resentments still linger in some areas, where someone from the south can still be termed a "Sassenach", a derogatory Gaelic term for a lowlander.

I remember watching the weather forecast one evening on the television. The map of southern Scotland flicked up with its usual mix of little rain clouds and suns. Only there was something missing—Edinburgh. Instead of placing the capital city on the map, the nearby towns of Haddington and Kirkcaldy were clearly marked. The most logical explanation is that the programme's producers are based in Glasgow and someone there would rather forget that Edinburgh ever existed!

The east and west of Scotland is also divided by old rivalry. The two principle cities are forever competing for political and cultural ascendance. Most Glaswegians would prefer the new Parliament and the capital city to be in their hometown. Likewise folk from Edinburgh secretly wish their city had a bit more of Glasgow's buzz.

Jealousies such as these are light hearted and make for plenty of jokes and comparisons. People from Edinburgh usually end up being portrayed as being cold and arrogant or "snooty" and the Glaswegians as being just plain mad, or "mental." The rivalries don't end there. Traditionally there is little love lost between Glaswegians and Aberdonians, although I have no idea why. Perhaps this once tribal society has just always needed a neighbour to compete with.

Chapter Three

DO YOU KEN?

"Ah burrit Faither in the sand
Mither opent the picnic
An made us a' piece an chicken roll
-it wis braw-"
—Opening stanza of *The Beach* by Iain Harvey

The Scots are great communicators and it's hardly surprising that they
have developed rich forms of expression. Not only does Scotland
have its own dialect with a lot of regional variety in accents and
expressions, it also maintains its own native language: Gaelic.

Being Scottish is closely tied up with the accent. Speak with a
Scots accent and it doesn't really matter where you are originally

from. So if you can pick up some of the local expressions and intonations you will get that much warmer a reception. Scots is a beautiful and rich dialect that graces any foreign tongue well. I don't think I've heard a sweeter accent than from a Swedish girl who mixed up Irish, Swedish and Scots accents into a unique whole.

Note that not all Scots have Scots accents. There are those who grew up abroad and moved back but there are also true natives who don't have a Scots tinge. Most of these went to one of the country's private schools where the Queen's English is traditionally taught, rather than the local dialect.

GAELIC

Scotland's indigenous language isn't English, it's Gaelic. Gaelic is the language of the Celts and came from Ireland in the 6th century. Right up until the beginning of the 20th century Gaelic was commonly spoken across much of Scotland. However with the introduction of compulsory schooling in the nineteenth century the language was actively discouraged and carried the stigma of being thought of as backwards and simple until relatively recently. In Ireland, Gaelic or Irish speakers as they are termed used to be called "bog hoppers"; rural types cut off from the modern world.

I remember as a boy hearing Gaelic spoken more than English by the old people on the west coast. Like a gentle rain its soft lilt always fascinated me. Although we did have a few hours of Gaelic taught to us a week at school, for most of our generation it was a case of too little too late. Gaelic spoken as a first language has been eroded back to the small islands like Harris and Lewis. The sense of its loss is still palpable to many, such as the poet Kenneth C. Stephens who wrote:

> "On Iona, the last Gaelic speaker has died…
> …All over the Western Islands the last ones are going
> like candles at night, falling across the wind
> their last words lost and drowned in time."

Gaelic may no longer be a commonly spoken language in Scotland, but it has enjoyed something of a revival in recent years. Gaelic speaker Paddy Shaw who lives outside the small village of Awe near Oban is encouraged by initiatives to keep the language alive. "There is a real resurgence going in the cities, with Gaelic medium schools, the Gaelic radio station *Radio nan Gaidheal* in Inverness and Gaelic television," Paddy told me. Much of the television is pitched toward children, who can now watch Gaelic versions of cartoons such as *Danger Mouse*, where the hero is renamed Donnie Murdo.

In Edinburgh there are moves to make Gaelic part of the political lexicon. Some of the debates in Parliament are now being held in Gaelic. Although few on either side of the political divide speak fluent Gaelic, the initiative is an important recognition of what was Scotland's first language up until a couple of centuries ago.

Outside of the cities there are also promising signs that Gaelic has a real future in Scotland. In the beautiful setting of Sleat in southern Skye a Gaelic college has been running for some thirty years now. Called "a big shed" or *Sabhal Mor Ostaig*, the college is an important centre for anyone who wants to learn Gaelic, as well as being renowned for its late night sessions of folk music. There is also a Gaelic summer camp, called the Feis, for children on the islands of Tiree and Barra.

The biggest date in the calendar for Gaelic speakers is the Mod (the meeting). Organised by the Gaelic society, the Mod is a competitive festival of music, song, storytelling and dance that is held in early October in towns across Scotland. The Gaelic choirs are a high point at these festivals, which used to be a normal part of village life. Their strongholds are now in Argyll and the island of Barra.

There is hope for the survival of Gaelic as a living language. "More and more folk want to learn Gaelic and people like myself who speak the language are no longer looked down on, we are more envied or respected," said Paddy Shaw. But the survival of the language, so important to Scotland's cultural diversity, still hangs in the balance.

"It's children that hold the future of the language. The problem is that when children become teenagers they often loose interest and move away from the Gaelic scene," said Paddy.

SPEAK SCOTS

The Scots accent is one of the most distinctive in the English language, and according to most Sean Connery fans, one of the sexiest. However Scots is much more than an accent. It's a dialect, rich in its own words and expressions.

A few hundred years ago the English language in Scotland was so peppered with local expressions and phrases that "Scots" was virtually a language in itself. Just read some of the 18th century poet Robert Burns' work and you will see how many of his words need translation. In school students study "Burns speak" to bring his poetry properly to life. There are several meticulously researched Scots dictionaries that cast light on many of the words that have since passed out of use.

There are still plenty of Scots phrases and expressions that can give an added dimension to speaking English in Scotland. Whether it's saying "aye" instead of "yes", "wee" instead of "small", or "tattie" instead of "potato", there is a host of new words even the most fluent of English speakers who visit or live in Scotland would have to learn.

Fifty years ago there was an enormous amount of variety in accents and dialects across Scotland. Every area had a distinctive voice and set of colloquialisms. None more so than Glasgow that was so rich in local words and sayings that the dialect is known as "the Glasgow patter." With less people spending their whole lives in one village or valley many of these regional distinctions have begun to be evened out.

But there are still big variations. For example the accent on the west coast of the Highlands is softer and more singsong, reflecting the number of Gaelic speakers there for whom English was a second language in the past. Scots from rural Aberdeenshire in the Northeast have such a strong dialect that they can be particularly hard to follow. The accent from the lower Clyde is famous for its breakneck pace and bewildering mix of local expressions. The small islands can also have very distinctive accents. For example people from Orkney (called Orcadians) have an unmistakable way of speaking. Their accents sound closer to Welsh than Scottish.

Swearing in Scots

Anyone who has ever learned a foreign language knows that the first words you pick up are usually the worst ones. There are plenty to get started with in Scotland. The most common expletives are "fuck" and "shit", pronounced "shite." But there are more imaginative ways of expressing yourself with swear words, and of being insulting. Someone can be a "dickhead," "prick," "bastard," or "wanker." To emphasise the point put "fucking" beforehand.

The word "bastard" can be used to describe a person, thing or situation. One friend from Spain has only been learning English in Scotland for a few months heard the word so much that she took to using bastard before naming anything from a mountain to a cup.

Much of the swearing in you may hear in Scotland doesn't have bad intent. In Glasgow it is so common that even the strongest of four lettered words (c***) has become a common term. So don't be surprised if you ask someone there for directions and they say, "Aye well you see that road there, follow the c*** down to the light and turn left…" This can cause confusion. Jamie Kenny, a young lad from Glasgow was in the marines in the south of England but had to drop out because he got into so much trouble. He would go out for a few drinks and get into fights with the locals because all that they understood from his Motherwell accent was a string of expletives.

Abusive hand signals in Scotland and in Britain in general are the first and index finger held up with the palm pointing inwards. Even stronger is the index finger alone. These signs are used jokingly between friends but are seldom seen in public. They are most commonly put to use in traffic, when frustrated drivers flash the V's at aggressive drivers before speeding off to escape the consequences.

You might think from all this that the Scots are a foul-mouthed people who love cussing. This couldn't be further from the truth. Most are very careful about their language, especially in front of strangers.

HOT CONVERSATION TIPS

British people are masters at idle chitchat and can while away hours saying nothing in particular. They tend to avoid talking about their real feelings, especially with strangers, so this kind of light conversation is a way of being friendly without being revealing. It is more noticeable south of the border where people tend to be more inhibited, but it is also relevant to Scotland, especially with the older generation.

Stepping into the social scene for the first time can be bewildering. Lucy Hunt, who moved to Scotland in the 1970s from Boston, first encountered the famous British reserve at a meal out with Scottish acquaintances. "They spent the first half hour talking about the weather," she said, " before rounding on price rises in the supermarket." Deciding that conversation needed a little bit of a boost she attempted to move on to a passionate discussion about the political situation. The response was stunned silence—she had committed her first of many social faux pas.

In formal social environments or sit down dinners, religion, politics, and sex are off the agenda. This is particularly true of the upper classes, where it is positively de rigueur to act a bit thick. Coming from an academic background where ideas and debate are valued, Lucy was often lost and somewhat bored. She has since learned the delicate art of small talk, filling silences by talking about things that are neither personal, nor potentially contentious. "I feel I am just making a series of friendly noises, it's not what I would call a real conversation, but it does smooth the way," she says.

Younger Scots are much more vocal about what's on their mind. But when dining with strangers, it's safest to start with suitable general subjects such as the weather (in a maritime climate there is always something to say!) and see where that takes you. It's hard to pin down what young people like to talk about, as they are generally happy to chat about anything once they get started. If you follow the football or the rugby it can be a head start, particularly when chatting with men.

If that fails, recent films, what has been on television or what your plans are for the night or the weekend are also good conversation topics. Scots are generally more politicised than the English and are much informed and comfortable with discussions on the events of the day. They also tend to be more left wing in their outlook.

If all else fails there is always that old gripe, the English. The Scots still love to complain about their poor treatment at the hands of their southern neighbours. Although there is perfectly good justification for this lingering bitterness, it's also true that it's easier to blame someone else for your troubles than deal with them yourself. The new Scots Parliament and political devolution have brought with them a more positive attitude and now the negative talk about "the English" is decreasing.

Body language

Rebecca Castro, who moved to Scotland from Chile a year ago, is used to seeing more physical affection between friends. "I've made good friends here," she told me, "but I find it strange that the Scots aren't as touchy-feely as people are in warmer climes."

In Chile no one escapes a "hello" or "goodbye" without a kiss on the cheek or a hug. In Scotland a "hello" or "goodbye" comes with a handshake and often just a nod. Friends can say goodbye for a long parting and muster little more than a particularly rigorous handshake. Touching and kissing is generally restricted to sexual relations, particularly amongst older generations

The space between two people speaking is also important. The British have a keen sense of personal space so it's best to keep your distance. If someone leans into your face while speaking to you in Scotland it usually means that they either want to kiss you or are making a strong case for breaking both your arms.

Body language in Scotland is often contained. People don't swagger around unless drunk and seldom gesticulate with their hands. Likewise the volume of conversations is lower than in countries like Chile or Italy. Step into a café in Scotland and you may notice that people tend to speak in muted toned compared to the Italians or Spanish who seem to be constantly arguing to the British ear.

But this isn't the whole story. In a bar much of this caution drops away. With an easy flow of drink the Scots open up to friends and strangers alike. At a ceilidh they are whirling dervishes, spinning and cantering around the dance floor with ease. But these are controlled environments where it's accepted to throw away inhibitions (with the odd drink). Social inhibitions are being worn away by new generations of Scots that travel and bring back more "southern" and relaxed attitudes and customs to Scotland. Rebecca hopes that, "they will pass this more relaxed expression of feelings to their kids, and that the culture in Scotland will come to allow them a freer way to express themselves in public."

— *Chapter Four* —

FITTING IN

"May the best ye've ever seen
Be the worst ye ever see."

—Traditional toast

To those used to the hustle of a big metropolis, Scotland's principal urban sprawls can take a little getting used to. The nation's capital Edinburgh is a good example. Coming from the mad rush of London, called "the city that never sleeps," Edinburgh has a flavour not unlike a small town in Spain or Italy. Life is much more laid back. In the summers the meadows in the parks are filled with sun worshippers, amateur footballers, Frisbee fanatics, and the unfortunates who have to make it to work but don't seem in any particular hurry to get there.

In the winters the Scots settle into the long cold nights and short cold days with ease. Like a squirrel in winter's icy grip they also seem to retreat into semi-hibernation. The windswept streets become places to dash along between work, home, a bar, or a crowded café. In London or New York a café is a place to snatch a cappuccino before appointments, or just to be seen with your designer clothes, sunglasses and mobile phone. In Edinburgh or Glasgow, café life is about relaxing, chatting with friends or whiling away an afternoon with a book and your own thoughts. Outside of the cities and towns, life is even more relaxed (see chapter eight).

MANNERS

Mind your Ps and Qs

Being polite is very important in Scotland. The Scots pride themselves on their hospitality and friendliness, and are generally cautious and respectful of their fellow human beings. "Please," "thanks pal," and "sorry" punctuate most conversations. If you bump into someone it's likely that they will fire off an apology before you do.

A reputation for good manners is common to the British Isles. While people in the south of England can be very courteous, they can lack the sincerity of the good-humoured friendliness of the Scots. At least that is the perception of Penny Travlou, a Greek national who has lived in both England and Scotland over the past six years. "I think that the Southerners (from southern England) are polite without meaning it, but the Scots really do mean it," she said.

Just Say No

The British in general and the Scots in particular find it hard to say a direct "no." If asked a favour they will say "maybe" even when they would rather not. This inability to say "no," is most common with invitations. Few will initially turn down an invite, be it for a party or a holiday. Only later, they may end up making their excuses or just not turning up. Generally they didn't change their mind, they just didn't want to offend in the first place.

In general the Scots and the British are also quick to make vague promises to "come round," "get together," or "see you tomorrow," before quickly forgetting about it. This is just a polite way of saying "goodbye" and can be very confusing to the unsuspecting foreigner. I had one poor German friend who actually waited in for a couple of weeks because some people she met had said they would "pop round to visit soon." They never showed.

The trick is managing to tell when "yes" actually means "probably not" and when agreeing to meet again ("See you soon") is actually a polite way of saying "Goodbye for now." Classic phrases that say "yes" but usually mean the opposite are, "Oh aye, that sounds nice," or "That sounds interesting," or "I'll have to think about it." The Scots, masters of understatement when they want to be, will often damn an idea or project with faint praise rather than condemn it to your face.

Public Reserve, Private Space

The Scots are at heart a reserved people. As friendly as they may be to strangers, it takes time to get beyond the banter and make genuine friends. Penny Travlou saw this odd contradiction first hand when she came from Greece to live in Glasgow. "Glasgow still has something of a community feel to it," she told me. "If you wait at a bus stop someone will definitely talk to you... But my biggest frustration when I first came was making friends."

Penny found that it was harder to gain the trust and confidence of Scottish people compared to those in Greece. "In Greece you can meet people and socialise with them easily, but it doesn't mean that they will become close friends... here people need time to feel relaxed and comfortable with you, but once you get to know them, they make excellent friends," she said.

This reserve is most evident when it comes to the home. "Home is where the heart is" goes that most overused of British expressions. It's a cliché because it is so true. Just look at the energy put into most gardens in Scotland or leaf through an *Ideal Homes* magazine and you get some idea of the love, care and attention that most put into their living spaces.

Someone's home is an intimate and very private expression of himself or herself. So it's best not to pop round to someone's house or flat without an invitation if you don't know them too well. "It's strange, home is a private castle here," says Penny. "When I first came I used to drop in on people uninvited and feel like I was invading, now I phone beforehand to give some warning."

Talking About the Weather

The weather in Britain is an obsession. You only have to listen to Radio 4's *Shipping Forecast* to get a sense of the place the weather has in the heart of the British nation. The names listed in the forecast circling the coast of Britain are timeless and unchanging. Delivered in a clipped English accent, the voice is soothing even when it warns of gales and storms.

The best icebreaker in most conversations is to pass a comment on the weather. It's a way of making an extended "hello" and it oils the wheels of social interaction. Since the weather is so unpredictable, there is always something new to remark on.

For example, much like the Arctic Inuit people's 100 names for snow, the Scots have a myriad of different ways of describing their national affliction: rain. It can be raining, showering, pissing it down, pouring, spitting, drizzling, misty, or just a wee bit wet. Perhaps only a native would be able to differentiate between "Showers sometimes heavy" and "Persistent rain."

The next best bet to commenting on the weather is to make a feeble attempt at the impossible—a prediction. Actually how accurate you are is irrelevant, it's more about making the right noises.

COPING WITH THE WEATHER

Talking about the weather in Scotland is the easy part, you then have to survive it. Amber from Australia lived through a winter in Dundee dreaming of surfing the waves on the beaches outside her hometown of Sydney. "I missed the heat back home sooo much," she told me, "there were days when the wind was so strong that I used to just scream at it with frustration."

If you're from a hot country, the weather can take time to adapt to. My Spanish friend Nacho complained that it isn't the winters that are so bad, he expected them to be long and dark. It was the cool damp summers that followed after he had survived the winter that he found the hardest.

Spring can be the cruellest. In March the daffodils push themselves reluctantly out of the soil, the cherry trees burst into bloom and there is the first whiff of cut grass as lawn mowers get dusted off to trim long dormant lawns. Days lengthen, the sun pops out, and you can be forgiven for breathing a deep sigh of relief and rejoicing that spring is here—at last.

Don't bet on it though. As often as not the winds and cold return their icy grip overnight, throwing the country back into winter for a spell. It's as though the god of weather is one of those dour Presbyterian ministers who frowns on anything less than hard work and suffering. "Aye well you've had your fun, now that's it! Get back inside and back to work, your punishment isn't over yet you bunch of snivelling sinners!"

However the weather isn't as bad as you may have been led to believe. Scotland suffers from the many myths of a cold country. Nacho was told before he arrived that if the curtain touched the window during a Scottish winter, it would freeze and break off. He arrived in December to be pleasantly surprised at how mild it was compared to his dire expectations.

There is also more sun around than you might expect. On a hot day in southern Scotland the thermometer can peak at 30° C. A common complaint further North is that the weather forecasters constantly leave a dark cloud hovering over them on the map, even when it's a beautiful sunny day.

There is also a real magic to the weather's capricious turns. A day can start with rain, turn to hail, snow, and sleet before brightening up for a glorious afternoon. One friend reasons that the weather goes a long way toward explaining the Scots' ingenuity and quick wit. Constantly kept on their toes by the continual swing of the barometer, they adopt something of its fast-moving spirit.

DRESS SENSE

Dress sense in Scotland is far from exotic. Little thought is given to style outside of Glasgow, where young people in particular sport casual designer wear. In most of Scotland the dress code is pretty flexible, depending, of course, on the weather. The notable exception is the club scene when sleek young things dress in the finest fashions. Older people take more care with their appearance and tend to be well turned-out in neat, if a little sombre, attire.

Oddly enough, this lack of attention to what you are wearing can be refreshing, particularly for people from countries like Italy or Spain, where so much time is spent in front of the mirror. Penny is thankful: "The Scottish can be terrible dressers with no sense of fitting things together, but on the other hand you feel more comfortable here. You can dress casually and you don't have to wake up in the morning and say, 'Oh my God what am I going to wear!'," she said.

Times are changing, as the restless Western desire for eternal youth and the body beautiful catches up with Scotland, albeit slowly. According to a spokeswoman from Transform, the largest UK company that specialises in plastic surgery, there was a 20% growth in the industry in Scotland between 1988–1999. Over 40% of this "corrective surgery" was for breast enlargements. However Scotland has a long way to go before it matches Brazil or Argentina in the plastic surgery stakes. For the time being, most teenagers and twentysomethings are content to settle for the odd skin piercing—a metal ring or studs in the tongue or belly button.

Tartan Times

Traditional Scottish dress is more and more in vogue, especially with young people. Scotland's trademark, the tartan, is worn at weddings, funerals, Highland balls, posh nights out, and sometimes just for a few beers in the local pub. The tartan is made up from different coloured yarns and woven together to produce a multicoloured check, called a "sett." Each clan name has a number of distinctive patterns or setts to choose from.

It is only since the 17th century that specific tartans have been reserved for family names or clans. But the tartan has been an insepa-rable part of Highland dress for centuries. Look at the colours of the Highlands in any season and you will understand where much of the inspiration comes from. In the autumn for example, the stag grass seems on fire in deep orange, the bracken beside it is a rich rusty brown and the Rowan tree berries add a bright splash of red.

The colours once came from the very plants they reflected. There are hundreds of plants that give good colour in Scotland. Some of the most important are the lichens, which give a wide range of rusty oranges, as well as rich purple when soaked in ammonia (urine!). The myrtle provides deep greens, iris gives black, and yellow can be made from many plants.

Technically it is only fitting to wear tartan if you have a clan surname, either on your mother or your father's side. However, if you can't claim clan ancestry, do not despair. Since most patterns are relatively recent inventions, you can always invent your own. For example, the racehorse Red Rum had his own tartan made especially for him.

Tartan is most typically worn as a kilt. The kilt, based on the premise that knees are an erogenous zone, needs no introduction. Legend has it that nothing is ever worn underneath a kilt although the

Father and son team up in tartan.

cold, midges, and a revealing spin at a ceilidh can make for strong disincentives. Other options are the drainpipe tartan trousers or "trews" for men and a tartan sash worn over an evening dress for the ladies.

Kilts aren't cheap to have made up, costing around £300 each. But they are a lifetime investment, with a few extra inches measured into the girth for lateral growth in years to come. It is possible to rent kilts, although it is hard to find the lesser-known tartans. Most Scots have their own kilts made up and rent the rest of the clobber for around £40 a night. This includes a tweed or Argyll jacket for casual wear or a smart Prince Charlie jacket for more formal occasions. There is the ubiquitous leather pouch or sporran round the midriff, coming in all shapes, sizes, and with all variety of animal hairs. Footwear is a pair of distinctive ghillie brogues and long socks with a small black knife, known by its Gaelic name of "sgian dubh."

GOING OUT

Drinking

Dimitris came to Edinburgh to study at the Herriot Watt University for three years. Born and raised on the island of Corfu, he knew something of the British drinking culture from seeing the yearly invasions of holidaying Britons to his island in the summers. He didn't think much of their habit of getting steamingly drunk and collapsing on the beaches every night. But he thought they were just letting off steam while on holiday

On moving to Scotland to study he was surprised to discover that the British habit of drinking to drunken excess isn't reserved for holidays. He saw the same spectacle of staggering groups, spilling out of one bar or another on a Friday or Saturday night barely able to make their way home.

"In Greece," Dimitris told me, "drinking that much is frowned upon. It's not acceptable to loose control like that and make such a fool of yourself."

In Britain drinking to excess is not only acceptable amongst the young, it is virtually expected of young men. If you go to a bar and drink nothing but Coca-Cola through the night, you'll be met with mild disapproval. Real men and women are supposed to drink beer after beer from pint glasses. This is often topped off by a bruising round of spirits.

Compared to Mediterranean countries which mix dancing, eating, and drinking in even measure, Britain has much more of a beer culture. Scotland has more civilised licensing hours with bars staying open well into the night. In England the pubs close at 11:00 pm, so drinking tends to be squeezed into a few frenzied hours between early evening and closing time.

Drinks are often bought in rounds, so if you go out as a group everyone is expected to buy everyone else a drink at some point. Over the course of an evening, this can all add up to a lot of alcohol and it's not uncommon to see men and women staggering home blind drunk at the end of a night out; singing, shouting, or fighting as they go along their merry way.

It's accepted behaviour in Scotland, a chance for people to let go of their social inhibitions and throw caution to the wind. After living some years in Scotland, Penny Travlou remains bemused. "It's as though the Scots show another self every Friday night that isn't reserved, controlled, or even rational."

Parties

House parties happen all the time in Scotland. They are thrown to celebrate birthdays, moving into a new place (called a house or flat warming), to say goodbye to someone or sometimes for no particular reason at all. House parties follow predictable lines: booze, chat, and a little dancing. The dancing generally comes last on the agenda.

People are expected to bring drinks with them although the host also provides something, usually a lethal punch that virtually corrodes through the plastic cups it is poured into. Whereas in some countries everyone puts booze onto a communal table and helps themselves to whatever they fancy, in Scotland guests can be a little protective over their drinks, so be wary of drinking someone else's.

Occasionally, house or flat parties have "fancy dress" themes. This means that you are expected to dress up in ridiculous clothes and be good-humoured about it. There is no shame in this and many partygoers go to great effort and expense to come up with inventive costumes. I remember a James Bond theme party where one man turned up dressed as an underwater frogman, complete with wet suit and scuba diving tank!

Dinner parties are much more formal affairs. Once you have accepted an invitation it is rude to not turn up, or to show up more than half an hour late. Expect to bring a bottle of something (usually wine) and although there is no need to send a thank you note, a telephone call to say thanks is welcome and it is polite to return the favour some time in the near future. The Scots have a keen sense of reciprocity when it comes to invitations.

Saying grace before eating is common amongst Scotland's God-fearing citizens. This can be a simple "Thank you for the food that is about to be eaten," or a longer prayer to cure the ills of the world. There is nothing more embarrassing than being told that it is time to say grace after you have already started your soup. So it is best to delay starting the meal until you know what that household's etiquette is regarding grace.

Flirting

Flirting is in some ways a much subtler affair in Scotland than in many other cultures. Men in particular tend to be shy when it comes to approaching, or "chatting up" a woman. Penny comes from Greece where men are much more direct, and is often confused. "Men can be shy and have this terrible fear of rejection," she told me. "You don't have any idea how someone feels about you and end up trying to guess." Whereas in countries such as Italy, it is understood that men will make comments about women in the street, in Scotland it's a privilege reserved for workmen.

Alcohol loosens tongues and gives men and women an excuse to relax and flirt. Scots are much more forward when they are drunk. They can have a one-night stand and justify it as: "Oh I was drunk" the next morning. There is a strong sense of monogamy within relationships and although affairs happen they are less socially acceptable than in some other cultures.

A Note on Saunas

If you're in Edinburgh and fancy a quick sauna to ease the cold from your joints think twice. Most saunas are fronts for brothels. Although it's officially illegal to run brothels in Scotland, in Edinburgh the police turn a blind eye, reasoning that it's safer for all concerned to keep the oldest of professions behind closed doors. Elsewhere in Scotland, prostitutes remain on the streets.

This can lead to confusion if caught unawares. Jeannine came over to stay from France and saw a job advertisement for a "sauna assistant," in the local paper. Thinking that it would mean showing clients around and keeping the place neat and tidy she called up to inquire. The owner got very excited when he heard her French accent on the phone and asked her for her height and vital statistics. Confused, Jeannine asked just what the job entailed as it hadn't been very specific in the advertisement. "Oh," the man replied, "just massage and a little extra." She hung up.

RELIGION

Ever since the Protestant Reformation back in the 17th century, religion has been a contentious issue in Scotland. Catholics and Protestants have been at each others' throats for centuries, an old divide still mirrored in sectarian tensions in the southwest of Scotland. Most Scots are Protestant (Church of Scotland or Free Church) with a Catholic minority.

In recent years a growing immigrant population has brought a rich diversity of religions and creeds. Even religions that are usually associated with Asian or Middle Eastern countries, such as Islam and Buddhism, are now well represented.

Religion used to play a seminal role in Scottish society. In the 18th century the Presbyterian church, or Kirk, had a say in most aspects of public and private life.

Amongst older people and in the more isolated areas of Scotland, the Free Church, or "Wee Free," as well as other Christian denominations, still hold a lot of authority (see chapter nine). For younger Scots though, it is a different story.

Although religious education is still compulsory in school the idea of going to church on a Sunday has lost much its appeal in an increasingly secular society. Young people are more likely to turn to non-conventional sources of spiritual wisdom, if they take an interest in religion at all.

There is a growing Green or "New Age" movement in Britain, with many people getting connected to less conventional belief systems such as earth goddesses and eastern philosophies.

In Scotland there is also a revival of interest in old pagan practices. According to work by Professor Ronald Hutton of Bristol University the number of pagans in Scotland has increased from a mere handful in the 1940s to around 12,000 today. Students in Stirling can now study the healing powers of witches in their degree courses. The old fire and brimstone ministers of the past must be turning in their graves—over 1,000 people accused of witchcraft were burnt in Scotland in the past.

Homosexuality
Homosexuality is generally more accepted in Scotland than it used to be. Gay men and women can be more open about their sexuality now than even ten years ago and there are well-established gay scenes in the big urban centres.

However prejudice does exist. When the Parliament in Westminster voted at the beginning of the millennium to repeal section 28, an outdated piece of legislation that outlawed "the acceptability of homosexuality as a pretended family relationship" in schools, there was a strong reaction in Scotland. The different churches united in their opposition to the move, with considerable support from the more conservative sectors of society. The legislation was passed regardless, but the whole episode seemed a throwback to the days when the church in Scotland tightly monitored and controlled questions of sexual conduct and perceived morality.

Racial Tolerance

Coming from big multicultural centres such as London or New York, Scotland can seem very "white" to outsiders. Walk around Edinburgh, Aberdeen, or any of the smaller cites and there don't seem to be many foreigners living in Scotland.

Scotland certainly lacks the dynamic mix of peoples that can make England, particularly London, such an exciting fusion of cultures. There is a fantastic variety of food, music, literature, and language, together with a remarkable degree of acceptance of these differences on all sides in cities such as London or Birmingham.

The flow of different ethnic and racial groups into Scotland may be lagging behind the south, but this is changing fast. Nowhere is this more evident than in Glasgow, where there is a growing Asian community. The old stereotype of the pale Scotsman or woman is breaking down. Nowadays in Glasgow you're just as likely to see a woman of Indian descent, dressed in a sari saying "Hiya," in a thick Glaswegian accent.

However the influx of immigrants and asylum seekers in recent years is causing resentment. There has been a spate of racially motivated attacks in Glasgow as well as increased levels of racial harassment, particularly towards refugees. There has been a similar pattern in Edinburgh. One black African was "glassed" outside a club by a passing group of strangers and needed more than 50 stitches to his face. Scotland's reputation for being a hospitable and tolerant society is being put to the test.

KEY RITUALS

Growing Up

The major birthdays in the passage to adulthood occur at the ages of 18 and 21. They are usually big celebrations and often come with big presents from the parents, such as a first car or a crate of expensive wine that has been put aside for years to mark the occasion.

For those who make it, graduation from university is also a seminal moment in most young adults' lives. It marks the end of student life and entry into the world of work. Graduation is a matter of pride for the whole family, and it is common to see portraits in living rooms of sons or daughters on graduation day, together with their beaming parents.

Tying the Knot

Marriage, that most ancient of social institutions, is still respected in Scotland and remains one of life's important rites of passage for many. I know from experience that there is nothing more nerve-wracking and exhilarating than going down on bended knee to ask a girl for her hand in marriage.

Customs are changing however, and there are many couples in Scotland who prefer to marry late, or not at all. According to the Office of National Statistics, the number of single and never-married thirty-somethings in Britain rose from 969,900 in 1987 to 2.3 million in 1997. Cohabitation is more common as many people are put off by high divorce rates, now running higher than one in three in Britain.

To become legally married, you have to have your names recorded in the civil registrar. This is available at a civil registration office, a church or pretty much anywhere you like, provided there is a minister present. Once the marriage is legally recorded, the ceremony that follows is entirely a matter of choice. The ceremony can be Catholic, Protestant, Hindu or pagan. You can get hitched in a mosque, in the botanical gardens, or naked on a beach, although the climate is likely to make this last option too bracing an experience. Most choose to get married in a church.

The party afterwards is called a reception and is generally held in a country house, the town hall, or a huge tent or marquee in the parents' garden. Historic Scotland does a roaring trade in hiring out castles and old stately homes for weddings and receptions. Demand for most big venues is high, especially during the marriage season between March and October. So bookings have to be made up to a year in advance.

In Edinburgh a common choice is a civil service or reception at the city council. High up on the sixth floor, guests can look out over the nearby folly of stone and spire—the Caledonian Hotel—and to the Forth River's meeting with the sea beyond. But there is little time to reflect on the view. Arriving from the church the guests are generally keen to get down to the highlight of the wedding: the fabulous party after the ceremony.

They are seldom disappointed. No holds are barred in providing plenty for all at the dinner and dance after the wedding. The event tends to kick off with tall glasses of champagne to loosen the guests' reserve. Guests are seated at tables set with linen and silver, waiters hover, and all await the entry of the bride and bridegroom. The master of ceremonies, usually a man but not the bride's father, announces their arrival and the hall erupts into cheers and applause as the couple breeze in.

Seated at a long high table, the first round of wine is served to them and everyone has to wait for the bride and bridegroom to start each new course. The food is most commonly a buffet, usually with a wide choice of cold and hot foods including luxuries such as lobster, prawns and even caviar laid out on sumptuous platters.

With the serving of dessert, the wine is finished and the glasses replenished with champagne. This is followed by the speeches. The master of ceremonies leads this long-winded, often drink-sozzled, and sometimes embarrassing series of speeches and minor confessions. The keynote speech is the best man's. This is when the best friend of the bridegroom pulls a series of well-rehearsed skeletons out of the closet, retelling some of the more embarrassing moments in the bridegroom's life.

This can touch on anything from his dress sense in the old school days, his desperate antics as a single man and, of course, how he fell hopelessly in love with the bride. These can be tense moments for a bridegroom as he hopes the booze and the limelight don't go to his friend's head and his speech fall the wrong side of discretion. The meal ends with the cutting of the wedding cake, usually a heavy fruitcake in an elaborate multi-tiered design.

Having survived all this consumption and socialising everyone is then expected to loosen their belts and dance until the early hours. The bride and bridegroom start the dancing off with a solo number, to a few shed tears in the audience. Then everyone old and young alike joins in. The younger legs dance reels until the early hours.

The finale of a Scottish wedding is often the most revealing. With the drink finally taking its toll and most feeling exhausted from the day's hectic proceedings, people tend to drop their guard. The two families either hit it off really well, or can rub each other the wrong way, fostering grudges for years to come. Singles often make a play for a partner in the reception's last hours and many a fresh romance blossoms. It is commonly joked that the bridesmaids are guaranteed a snog (kiss).

Some time toward dawn everyone says their goodbyes and makes their way back to their hotel rooms none the wiser but one hell of a lot fuller than they had been the day before. The bride and bridegroom summon their last energies for the wedding night and the waiters eat the leftovers in the back kitchens.

All that's left is the colossal bill for the event, which can run into tens of thousands of pounds. It is traditionally the responsibility of the parents of the bride, with the exception of the drinks which can be paid for by the bridegroom's parents. The responsibility for the cost of the honeymoon generally falls to the bridegroom. It's not uncommon to see everyone but the bride's father having a whale of a time, while he surveys the scene with resignation and a bit of pleasure, pondering on the penury inflicted on him by a single night of revelry.

For young couples who don't have their parents consent, there is always Gretna Green. This nondescript Scottish town on the border with England is an odd choice for young couples from England to tie the knot. Under Scottish law, you don't need your parents' consent to get married past the age of 16, whereas in England parental consent is required, until you are 18. Commonly termed "Scotland's Las Vegas," Gretna Green is the nearest town to the border with England and for years has been a Mecca for young English lovers dashing north across the border to get hitched on the sly.

Gretna Green has since lost some of its popularity, although the hotels there still bulge with red-sequined and heart-shaped four poster beds to accommodate the romance of first love. The town itself is also famed for its nuclear submarines and is, in fact, a harsh environment for true romance to flower.

MYTH, LEGEND, AND SUPERSTITION

There are two worlds in Scotland, the seen and the imagined. The country is so steeped in myth and legend that if you delve too deeply into it the shadows can start playing tricks on your eyes. Most terrifying of all are the witches.

According to Scottish folklore there are witches everywhere, casting about their evil eye and constantly dreaming up some new mischief. Scotland's very own Blair Witch is said to reside outside of the small Perthshire town of Blair Atholl, on the mountain of Ben-y-Gloe. There she presides, eating snakes alive and, according to one account: "...driving cattle into morasses to die, riding horses by night till they drop from exhaustion. She can take the shape of a raven, eagle, or deer; she destroys bridges, and tempts people to fall into raging rivers by creating the image of floating treasures just out of reach." The Blair Witch sounds like she may have been one of the old hags that Shakespeare's *Macbeth* came across on some "blasted heath."

Witches are only one of the myriad of fairies, devils, brownies, and other mythical creatures that have been dreamt up, or reportedly seen in Scotland. Many are a mix of old Celtic and Norse legend, and this is not surprising for an island people intimately related to the sea. It isn't just mermaids that lure sailors into their watery paradise. The big grey seals that live off the shores have long been associated with the mythical selkies (meaning *seals* in Orcadian dialect), that occasionally come onto land and assume human form. No one agrees about whether they are fallen angels or humans cast out for previous sins. If you get a chance to watch seals draw near you in the gloaming (dusk) with their large liquid eyes gazing at you curiously across the water, you may find the old legend takes on fresh life.

Superstition

Of course the imagined world of myth and legend has been largely dispelled in modern day Scotland, but some of the old fears and beliefs remain. Superstition, ways of avoiding bad luck, the evil eye, or seeing portents of the future were traditionally rife in Scotland. For sailors in particular there was a whole series of complex do's and don'ts to ensure safe passage. For example, their wives at home would never blow on their soup to cool it, believing it would whip up a storm at sea.

The Scots still have a lingering respect for many superstitions. Just watch a flow of pedestrians carefully manoeuvring themselves around a ladder on a pavement rather than walk underneath it because it is considered bad luck.

Superstition is rarely talked about in Scotland, it is just taken for granted. There is a whole unwritten code, most of it changing from region to region or from family to family. For example, one Scottish friend would never break eggs without crushing them, or sign her name in red, in the firm belief that something bad would happen soon after.

She also told me never to look at a new moon through glass or the branches of trees and to watch out for crossed knives at the dinner table. If she caught a chill and shuddered she would go white and whisper, "I feel like a ghost just wandered across my grave." Her accent was strong, so I always heard "goose" instead of "ghost" and used to wonder what strange attraction geese had to the graves of the living.

Ghosts and Ghouls

Ghosts are never far away in Scotland; you will find many people who believe the country is seething with otherworldly spirits. "Centuries of warfare and bloodshed has left a multitude of restless souls lurking in Scotland's shadows," our ghost guide told us in the remains of Lady Mary's Close under the New Town in Edinburgh. The entire street was closed off some 400 years ago after an outbreak of the plague, its residents left to die either of the Black Death or of starvation. Afterwards the street became notorious for its ghostly apparitions and was later built over by the city council.

Tour companies take groups under the city streets to visit the long abandoned flats, complete with cobblestone streets once open to the skies. Whether or not you believe in ghosts, the sense of claustrophobia and time-locked anguish is almost overwhelming.

Scotland is full of ghost stories and its reputation for haunted vaults, graveyards, and castles is great for tourism. Room 109 in the youth hostel at Carbisdale castle in Sutherland is booked up weeks in advance because of its regular haunting. Called the Spook Room, children are said to run around at night in the old nursery moving beds and pouring water on the sleeping backpackers.

The Scots themselves are never short of a good tale or two. Telling ghost stories around a candle at night is something of a national pastime and no book about Scotland is complete without at least one spinetingler. My friend Conrad pulls this one out as his ace card just before everyone is about to go off to bed.

Conrad is a gardener. A few years ago he went to do some work on the garden of an old country house in the central Highlands. One weekend the owner was away and Conrad stayed on his own in the big house. Fearing a cold night he went into the basement and stocked up the boiler till the house was good and hot.

While quietly cooking in the kitchen in the evening, Conrad suddenly heard a girl call his name from somewhere in the house. He followed the call to see who it was, until he heard it again from the darkness at the bottom of the stars leading out of the basement. Somewhat shaken, he retreated to the kitchen to wait out the dawn.

When the owner came back Conrad told him about his experience, to which the reply was, "That will be the girl who is said to have burned to death some two hundred years ago. The house caught fire and she went back to her bedroom to fetch her teddy bear. She was last seen running through the house with her nightgown on fire. We still hear her occasionally."

FAMOUS MEN AND WOMEN

Here are some of the most important names to remember while you're in Scotland. Know a little about them and you can bluff your way through most high- or low-brow conversations.

Famous Figures of the Past

Saint Columba (521–597)—Sixth century Celtic firebrand who brought Christianity to the Pictish people and was buried on Iona.

Macbeth (unknown–1057)—King of Scots from 1040 who fought off the English only to be immortalised as evil incarnate in Shakespeare's play of the same name.

Sir William Wallace (1270–1305)—Patriot, national hero, and chief defender of Scotland's independence in the 13th century.

Robert the Bruce (1274–1329) or Robert VIII de Bruce—Actually an Anglo-Norman, Robert the Bruce tenaciously defeated English forces at the Battle of Bannockburn in 1314, ushering in a long period of independence for the fledgling Scottish nation.

Mary Queen of Scots (1542–1587)—Stuart queen whose tumultuous life, ending with her beheading at the order of Queen Elizabeth I, has something of the love, tragedy and fury of the country she has become a symbol for.

John Knox (1514–1572)—Protestant reformer and bitter enemy of the Catholic Mary Queen of Scots. Wrote *The History of the Reformation in Scotland*.

King James VI (1566–1625)—The first king of both England and Scotland, who styled himself "King of Great Britain."

Robert (Rob Roy) MacGregor (1671–1734)—Swashbuckling cattle thief who recently hit the big time in the film *Rob Roy*.

Bonnie Prince Charlie (1720–1788)—The Young Pretender. Made an audacious bid for the British throne with the Highlander's support in 1745, only to be defeated at the Battle of Culloden.

Flora MacDonald (1722–1790)—Scottish Jacobite heroine who helped Bonnie Prince Charlie flee the English after the Battle of Culloden. She has been immortalised in folk tales and songs ever since.

Robert (Robbie) Burns (1759–1796)—Scotland's best known poet and songwriter, whose words were almost as prolific as his womanising.

Sir Walter Scott (1771 – 1832)—Practised as a lawyer but famed as a poet and novelist. Best known are the Waverly novels, which include *Rob Roy*, *Ivanhoe* and *The Heart of Midlothian*.

Thomas Carlyle (1795–1881)—Historian and essayist who wrote on such epic themes as the French Revolution and Fredrick the Great.

David Livingstone (1813–1873)—The most famous of the wandering Scots. 19th century explorer who took on one inhospitable jungle too many, and also discovered Victoria falls.

John Muir (1838–1914)—He is considered the father of the modern environmental movement for saving Yosemite Park from lumber men in California's Sierra Nevada. The John Muir Trust was formed in 1985 to acquire and conserve wild land in Britain.

The Big Inventors—Scotland is famed for its inventive streak, particularly in medicine. To name a few, John Williamson found a vaccine for small pox, James Lind cured scurvy with lemons, Ronald Ross traced malaria to mosquitoes and Sir James Young Simpson discovered that chloroform is a great anaesthetic.

The Scots have been responsible for some big advances in modern technology. We must thank Alexander Bell for the telephone, John Logie Baird for pioneering the television, James Watt for inventing the steam engine and Sir James Dewar for coming up with the humble thermos flask. In 1996, scientists in the Roslin Institute outside of Edinburgh successfully cloned the first animal, Dolly the sheep.

Modern Day Celebrities

Robert Carlyle—Highly acclaimed actor who made his mark in the film *Trainspotting*, as well as playing lead roles in *Riff Raff, Carla's Song* and *The Full Monty*.

Robbie Coltrane—Actor and comedian, best recognised in the comic films *Nuns on the Run* and *The Pope Must Die*. Most recently seen on television in the dark detective series *Cracker*.

Sean Connery—007 agent with a licence to kill and break hearts. Ever popular with the ladies, he has appeared in plenty of films since his James Bond days but has never quite shrugged off the "shaken, not stirred" image.

Billy Connolly – Arguably Scotland's finest comedian. With a rich career on the stage and the big screen behind him, "The Big Yin" has come a long way since his *Great Northern Welly Boot Show* in the Edinburgh festival in the early seventies. He now lives in America.

Sir Alex Ferguson—Highly respected manager of Manchester United football club.

Annie Lennox—Pop diva from Aberdeen who, together with Dave Stewart, did much to lighten up a decade of outlandish hairstyles and crashing music.

Charles Rennie Mackintosh—Glasgow artist, architect and designer who is enjoying fresh fame for his stylish designs.

Shirley Manson—Edinburgh girl made good in the music world. Headed the bands Goodbye Mr Mackenzie and Garbage. Now based in America.

Ally McCoist—Called "Super Ally" by his fans, McCoist is famous for being a superb striker for Rangers and an all round nice guy. Now makes regular appearances on TV and still plays football.

Joe McFadden—Long standing actor in Scottish drama *Take the High Road,* also principle actor in TV adaptation of Ian Banks best-selling novel *The Crow Road.*

Ewan McGregor—Scots heart throb who is best known for his roles in the films *Trainspotting, Shallow Grave* and of course, *Star Wars: Episode 1.*

Eduardo Paolozzi—Edinburgh-based painter and sculptor of Italian descent who in recent years has become a household name.

Tommy Sheridan—Maverick leader of the Scottish Socialist Party and darling of the literary left.

Sir Jackie Stewart—Formula One world champion in 1969, 1971 and 1973. David Coulthard is the latest Scottish speed demon to grace the Formula One tracks.

Taggart—Dour Glaswegian police inspector of the long-standing series of the same name who is far tougher than the villains he tracks down. Most likely to say, "There's bin a murdur."

David Snedden—Young singer from Glasgow who has recently risen to fame after winning the *Fame Academy* television series.

— *Chapter Five* —

DOING BUSINESS

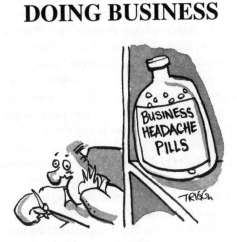

"Oh, it's nice to get up in the morning
And nicer to stay in bed."
    —Sir Harry Lauder , Scottish music-hall comedian,
                        singer, and songwriter.

THE PACE OF LIFE

In the old days of the Industrial Revolution, doing business in Scotland was a relatively straightforward affair. The big industries—mainly shipping, cotton, and jute—simply hammered and spun their wares for trade on the open seas.

Today the Scotland of the big yards, looms, and pits is remembered in albums of sepia photos for coffee tables. That isn't to say that the big industries are dead in Scotland, the yards on the north side of the Clyde still ring with the sound of construction. But labour-intensive industries have been in decline for a century, as the country increasingly adopts a service economy.

Many Scots still mourn the loss of some of the big industries, such as the Ravenscraig steel works in the 1980s, victims to the cold winds of free market economics and declining profits. Poverty and desperation brought on by higher unemployment has hit urban areas, such as Glasgow, hard. At football matches Partick Thistle fans still sing "You'll never work again" to rival fans from Motherwell, the area in Glasgow that supplied most of the labour to Ravenscraig.

The economy is now much more diverse, with many differing business interests working out of Scotland. For example, financial and business services now far exceeds engineering in employment. Edinburgh is an international centre for finance; the city ranks fourth after London, Paris and Frankfurt for international fund management.

The country's principal export is no longer iron or cotton, it is office machinery. The narrow strip of land between Glasgow and Edinburgh—known as Silicon Valley—produces over 30% of branded personal computers in Europe. The electronics industry employs over 40,000 people in computer and software manufacture.

Of course this isn't to say the advent of the brave new world of computers, international finance and the Internet marks the death knell of the old industries. Traditional businesses such as the fisheries, textiles, whisky, and more recently, oil and chemical manufacture, are still big sources of employment in Scotland's interdependent economy.

SOCIAL CUSTOMS

Before even contemplating the likes of paying taxes or setting up shop in Scotland, you need to know your way around the social landscape. How to relate to people in the business culture without making a fool of yourself is essential. It is, after all, a rigid environment where simple cultural misunderstandings can break down working relationships into embarrassment or worse still, high farce.

Both dress sense and body language are sombre in business environments in Scotland. Suits and dark colours carry the day, even a flashy kipper tie to offset the sea of navy blue and grey is too showy.

Introductions are equally formal. There is no physical contact beyond a round of handshakes and the odd pat on the back. It is important to look someone in the eye when you shake his or her hand and a good firm handshake is better respected than a limp one.

Whether meeting someone for the first or hundredth time, they will probably ask you how you are. This is a greeting, more of a rhetorical question than a general inquiry into your well being. The answer is invariably "Fine, thanks," or "I'm OK, thanks." There is no need to give any more detail.

Business cards should be given out sparingly and never on the first introduction. You have to gain your potential business colleague's confidence with some small talk before steaming in with business cards and contact phone numbers. Cards are usually given out after you have found common ground, not before.

Don't kiss or hug someone unless you know him or her very well or are very drunk. An Italian friend once sealed a deal at a board meeting with a kiss on the senior partner's cheek. In the stunned silence that followed he swore that his hair curled forever in embarrassment. In Scotland, men seldom kiss in public and certainly never at a business meeting.

The business world in Scotland doesn't have the cosmopolitan and international feel of big urban centres such as London or New York. The social circles in Glasgow and especially Edinburgh are more restricted, making them harder to break into.

The old school network, meaning the friends and contacts made from university and school days, is not as strong as it was 20 years ago. But the logic still persists that most prefer to do business with people they know. Many connections and big jobs are shared amongst ex-university colleagues who meet in smoky clubs to drink fine whisky, share out power, and generally think big.

Coming in from outside can be tricky to start with. For men, the old boys' clubs are nearly impossible to join unless you are nominated by one of the members. The best way to start meeting people is through sport. Golf is a popular meeting ground for businesses as you can both participate and talk shop. Remember that if you are playing golf you'll need a good handicap to keep pace in the country that invented it (see chapter eight).

For those who don't have the confidence, or the stamina, to streak around golf courses or football pitches, there are plenty of business forums, seminars, and networking lunches organised by the likes of the Chamber of Commerce. The Small Business Gateway Service, part of the Scottish Enterprise Network is also a good place to start meeting people. This government organisation has offices around Scotland and offers support to large and small businesses alike.

Scotland and Britain, in general, do not have the culture of the business lunch, so favoured in warmer, more laid-back countries. This doesn't mean that a three-hour boozy lunch is unheard of, but most settle for a sandwich in the office or a quick bite in a café.

A better bet for breaking the ice is a couple of drinks after work, although even this practice is surprisingly limited in Scotland. Apart from the ubiquitous few lost hours in the pub on a Friday evening, most scuttle home straight after work.

For women, the task of getting known and well connected is a little harder. An Australian businesswoman with years of business experience in Scotland said, "Although the business culture is not overtly macho, the old boys clubs and the sporting side is a harder nut to crack if you're not one of the lads."

There are organisations, such as the East of Scotland Women's Club that cater specifically to businesswomen, aiming to even up the balance a bit. But at the end of the day, women need just that little bit more guts to push themselves forward, especially in social situations.

The advantage of breaking into such a relatively small world in Scotland is that once your face is known—for better or for worse—the hard work is over. Make an impression on the social circuit and you're part of the crowd with your credibility (or lack of it) firmly established. Also, if you meet someone you think would make a valuable contact, you can be more or less assured that you will bump into them again. The same people inevitably come back round the merry-go-round of conferences and seminars.

Initially a little slow on the uptake in the Internet revolution, technological advances are now as much an aid to communication in Scotland as elsewhere in the business world. Most Scots have mobile phones and e-mail addresses.

PARLEZ VOUS ANGLAIS?

Language barriers can present serious problems in Scotland. Although most big companies have access to translation facilities, almost all business is conducted in English. Few Scottish business people are competent in foreign languages—there is little need when English has become such a universal means of communication.

Even if you speak fluent English, coming to terms with the Scottish accent can still be a challenge. Vicky, an Australian friend, has lived and worked in Scotland for a year and still struggles at meetings to understand the accents of some of the senior personnel. "I have problems with Glaswegians and Aberdonians and telephone conversations can be very tricky," she told me.

STRESS

Stress is a buzzword in Britain. In fact the word has virtually become a term for a medical condition in its own right, and covers a wide variety of symptoms. In London a day doesn't pass when you hear someone complaining that they are "sooo stressed out." But then working Londoners have to contend with long working hours, short lunches, and high-pressured deadlines. At the end of each long day they then have the pleasure of an average one-hour long commute home in a traffic jam or a sweaty underground train.

Scotland is a different story. The job market may not have the variety or the opportunities that London offers but working conditions are generally much more civilised. Office hours tend to be what they are said to be—usually from 9:00 am to 5:30 pm. Cities in Scotland are also smaller and less congested, making commuting to work less time consuming.

The business culture tends to be more laid back than elsewhere. A good gauge of this is in the national attitude to time. In the office environment further south every minute is precisely measured. If someone is late to work or to a meeting it usually has to be for a very good reason.

In Scotland, time is more accurately measured out in coffee spoons than in minutes on the clock. Meetings usually start late and it's acceptable to turn up five or ten minutes after the starting time. This more relaxed approach can be very frustrating if you are used to the business culture of countries such as Germany, which prides itself on good timekeeping.

Scotland may not have the same 110% Protestant commitment to long working hours as in other countries, but times are changing. As the computer revolution pulls businesses into the same virtual world of global commerce, life at work is getting faster paced. Increased traffic on the roads and rocketing house prices also contribute to a picture of longer work hours and increasing stress levels.

JOB HUNTING

Badly paid jobs are easy to find in Scotland. Much of the young work force is employed in hotels, cafés, call centres, and bars. Such jobs generally offer hard work, long hours, and wages that are rarely above the minimum wage of £3.70 an hour. Employees are often offered a few hours of part-time work a week, so that the employer is not obliged to give sick pay or other benefits.

Jobs such as these are advertised on the shop front window of the business, inviting people to apply within. They will expect to see your curriculum vitae (CV), the document listing your education, work experience, and references. Lower paid jobs are also advertised at job centres. These government buildings, where unemployed people apply for state benefits, have hundreds of positions on offer, most of them unthinkable. You have to apply to them through one of the job centres' staff.

Recruitment, or temping agencies also tender out work. This can be anything from silver service waiting at big functions to clerical work. The work offered can be on a permanent basis, or just a few weeks at a time. To find work with a temping agency, visit their offices in person with a CV and references. You will be given a short interview to determine your suitability and availability.

Higher wage brackets and more permanent positions are harder to find. These sorts of positions are most commonly found advertised in *The Scotsman* and *The Herald* on Fridays. It would also be worthwhile sending in a CV and covering letter directly to the Human Resources department of the company that you are interested in, asking for work.

To apply to an advertised job, start by sending in a letter asking for further information and an application form. Complete this and send it back before the deadline indicated on the job advertisement. In most cases you will be asked to include a CV and the addresses of two people willing to give references (known as referees).

If you are short-listed you will be asked in a letter to attend an interview. If you don't get this far you will usually receive a rejection letter. If you have an interview, phone first to confirm that you will be attending. Remember to dress formally on the day. A suit and tie for men and a smart dress or trousers for women is essential for most interviews. Some companies go on to ask for a second round of interviews or exhausting days of group assessment before a final decision is reached.

If you are chosen you will usually be phoned and offered the job. Should you choose to ask for some time to think about it, or even turn it down you are perfectly entitled to. Once you have accepted and signed a contract you are committed.

WHO'S TRADING?

The first step towards understanding how companies operate or set up shop in Scotland is to understand the different business forms. There are three main types:

Sole Trader

This is the easiest and quickest way to get started. You alone are responsible for the business, so you can either get rich quick or end up personally liable for a mountain of debt.

The advantages of a sole trader over other forms of business entities are that the paperwork is minimal, accounts are kept confidential and there is greater flexibility on tax payment. Converting a business into a limited company is also a relatively easy process, although transferring the ownership to another sole trader can be a bureaucratic headache.

Partnership

In a partnership two or more people arrange to share the responsibilities for the joint running of a business. The partners are jointly and severally responsible for any debts incurred by the business. This means that if one partner fails to cover his or her financial commitments, the other party or parties have to make up the shortfall.

The added risk is human. Partnerships, generally set up between friends, can end up being dissolved by bitter and impoverished enemies. It is therefore vital to draw up an agreement that clearly lays out each party's responsibilities to help avoid possible conflicts.

Limited Company

A limited company has a life of its own. It is a separate legal entity with directors and shareholders. Its main features are:

- The company is liable for its business debt, so shareholders can only lose the money they initially spent to buy shares. However, a lender may still ask for personal guarantees from directors, such as their house, as security on a loan
- It is easier to spread out or pass on the ownership of a Limited company and is therefore ideal for someone who wants to invest with shares without getting involved in day-to-day management.
- Income tax is only paid on salaries and perks. However National Insurance contributions are much higher for limited companies than they are for other business entities.
- A limited company has more credibility in the business world as records and accounts are obliged to be kept at Company's House for anyone to inspect should they wish to.

Cooperative and Community Businesses

Cooperatives are surprisingly popular in Scotland, and can be anything from building societies to bicycle shops. In a co-operative, the employees own the business equally and share in its running profits and losses.

A variation on the same idea is a community business, owned by a group of people with the same interests who live in the same area. A good example of this is the community buyout of the island of Eigg on Scotland's west coast in 1997. Fed up with a series of absentee landlords, the local inhabitants formed the Isle of Eigg trust and, with the help of the Scottish Wildlife Trust and the Highland Council, bought the island to manage themselves.

EMPLOYEES' RIGHTS

The numerous acts of Parliament, as well as European regulations concerning employment in Scotland makes it a complex area to understand. With Britain's ongoing integration into the European Union there are also bound to be more changes in coming years. For detailed and up-to-date information, it is best to contact the local Benefits Agency office or Citizens Advice Bureau.

Employment conditions in Scotland vary widely. Unless you are employed for less than one month, you are entitled by law to have your conditions of employment set out in a written statement, including the basics such as hours, holiday entitlement and pay.

The following basic working rights apply to all employees:

• According to European Law an employee can't be forced to work for more than 48 hours in a week. However an employee can work longer hours if he or she chooses to. This is agreed in a written statement with the employer that can be cancelled by the employee at any time in writing.

• Employees are legally entitled to join and take part in the activities of a trade union.

• The National Minimum Wage Act 1998 introduced a legal minimum hourly rate that must be paid to everyone 18 years old or over. The current rate for 18–21 year olds is £3.00, rising to £3.70 to those over the age of 21.

• Employers are obliged to provide sick pay to workers who are off due to illness. However the length of time and amount of money an employee is covered varies with each employer. The law concerning statutory sick pay is complex and open to interpretation.

"Throwing a sickie," or taking a day off from work with an invented ailment is a national pastime in Britain. These days, wary employers often ask for doctor's notes as proof that their sick employee is genuinely bedridden.

• If an employee is dismissed, he or she is entitled to a written statement giving the reasons for dismissal within 14 days. If an employee feels unfairly dismissed and has worked for 52 weeks or more, he or she can seek compensation in a tribunal. Claims must be made within three months, so it is important that you act quickly. Free legal representation, known as "legal aid," is not available at employment tribunal hearings. However, "legal advice and assistance" is. The Citizens Advice Bureau is the first port of call if you need to go down this road.

Maternity Leave

Maternity leave is yet another minefield of complex legislation. What is certain is that no woman can be dismissed on grounds of pregnancy or childbirth. If the pregnancy makes it impossible for the employee to carry out her duties, she can be suspended on full pay or assigned to another position within the company until after the child is born.

Pregnant employees are also entitled to time off work for antenatal care as well as paid maternity leave before and after the child is born. Provided the employee gives at least 21 days' notice (in writing) of her planned absence, her job must remain open for her to return after maternity leave.

It is illegal for an employer to allow a woman to return to work within the first two weeks of her giving birth and all women have the right to a basic 18 week maternity leave period. If the employee has been with the company for more than one year's continuous employment, she is entitled to an extended 29 weeks of leave, now called "additional maternity leave."

Paternity Leave

Fathers are finally being recognised in the law for their role in childcare. Any new dad who has been in continuous employment for at least one year is now entitled to at least 13 weeks' paternity leave for any child born or legally adopted after December 15, 1999. This leave is unpaid although increased pressure on the government to change this may bring results in the near future.

Fair Play

Women are by law entitled to the same pay as men for work of the same value. Under the Equal Pay Act of 1970, if there is a salary difference offered by an employer for the same job, it has to be justified by reasons other than gender. It is also unlawful to discriminate against women, or men for that matter, in the workplace. Due to European directives, this now includes the practice of positive discrimination, or deliberately employing either men or women to make up a better gender balance.

On an island that is increasingly becoming a melting pot of different peoples, there is sound legislation in place to protect Scotland's ethnic minorities in the workplace. Under the Race Relations Act 1976 it is unlawful to discriminate against a person on grounds of colour, race, nationality, or ethnic origins.

The Commission for Racial Equality—set up to give the above law teeth—helps employees who feel that they have been wronged for racial reasons. The Race Relations Act covers all forms of employment with the exception of work done in private households and work which would naturally require a person of a certain nationality or ethnic origin (such as Russian Cossack dancing).

THE TAX MAN

Resented across the land, the taxman is never far from any earnings or business ventures. The offices of the Inland Revenue produce lots of cheap and cheerful literature with smiling people explaining how fun it is to pay taxes. They don't fool anyone. The Inland Revenue is a labyrinth of departments, forms are complex and difficult to decipher, and there are heavy punishments if you are caught on the dodge. The following is a cursory glance of what lies in store for the potential employer or employee.

National Insurance

Whether you are an employer, employee or self-employed, you have to pay National Insurance and income tax towards your State Retirement Pension and other Social Security benefits. The amount due for National Insurance depends on how successful the business is, or your salary. There are several ways to pay National Insurance. Contact the local Department of Social Security office to negotiate which is best suited to you.

Pay As You Earn

If you employ someone, including yourself, you become your own tax collector. You are responsible for assessing and deducting income tax and National Insurance from your own or your employee's earnings. This money is deducted from an employee's net pay and then sent to the Inland Revenue. This system, known as Pay As You Earn (PAYE), applies to anyone earning more than £77.86 a week (from April 1997) for income tax and £62 a week for National Insurance.

On leaving a job you are entitled to claim back the tax that has been deducted if you have been on a low wage. The amount after which you can not claim tax back is currently around £4, 500 per annum, but this is revised regularly to keep pace with inflation.

Value Added Tax

Value Added Tax (VAT), currently 17.5%, is charged on most business transactions in the UK. VAT is charged on all goods and some services that are imported into the country.

VAT is not levied on everything. Some of the exceptions are professional training, some types of insurance, non-luxury foods, newspapers, books, children's clothing, and new houses. Your local VAT office—in the telephone directory under Customs and Excise— can give up-to-date information on VAT's long-armed reach.

Where relevant, VAT (Value Added Tax), also known as output tax, is charged by most suppliers. However only companies that trade over a prescribed amount—currently a turnover of £47,000 in any 12-month period—have to register for VAT payment. Being VAT registered means that you are obliged to invoice your customers for an additional 17.5% of the original charge. A company whose turnover exceeds the minimum amount but doesn't register, may have to pay for the VAT it did not charge its customers.

An accountant is a great help when it comes to disentangling yourself from the VAT maze. Accountants give advice, help make claims to all allowances due, and make sure that records are accurately maintained.

Income Tax for a Sole Trader or Partnership

The tax year for income tax runs from April 6 to April 5. Sole traders and partnerships have to pay income tax on their annual profits, as shown in their annual accounts. They are expected to pay this tax in two instalments, on January 31 and July 31.

The Inland Revenue now operates a system of self-assessment. This means that you can calculate the taxes that you owe yourself, or you can ask the Inland Revenue to calculate it on your behalf. If a company makes a loss over the first four years of business, it may be able to recover some of the income tax that it has paid out.

Corporate Tax for a Limited Company

As a limited company you will be paying income taxes on wages to yourself—and any other employees—under the PAYE scheme mentioned above.

In addition to income tax, limited companies have to pay corporate tax on their profits. The rate of tax for companies with profits below £30,000 is currently 24%. Britain's corporate tax is 31% for companies that generate more than £30,000 of profit. If a company has previously been running at a loss it can set its profits against the previous three years losses, or carry them forward for future tax returns.

SETTING UP YOUR OWN BUSINESS

Nicolas Stepanopolus knows the ups and downs of setting up a small business first-hand. He came over to Scotland from his home country of Greece in 1997, fell in love with a local girl, and settled down.

Hating the idea of working for someone else, Nicolas decided to set up a café in Edinburgh with his Scottish friend Graham, selling fresh organic juices and Mediterranean food. The café, called Lianachan, after the Gaelic word for *wee meadow*, is a bright and simple place with high ceilings and wooden tables. Nicolas sits by a window seat flooded with light that catches the lazy curl of his cigarette smoke.

Taking in the peaceful scene you would never guess just how fraught the process of setting up the café has been. It has not been an easy road, bringing that first idea to life in brick, mortar, and frothy cappuccinos. The truth is that for both Nicolas and Graham, setting up their own business has been an exhausting and at times bewildering journey. Nicolas looks like he's blinking away the darkness after finally slaying the Minotaur and tracing the string back out of the maze—of paperwork.

"It was very very frustrating to organise all of these things; getting properly set up, signing all of these papers and all the money, money, money that disappears to all these people," he explains.

To set up a business in Scotland you need money, patience and a lot of ink. There is a whole host of expenses, legal requirements and forms to be filled with financial penalties for those who don't comply.

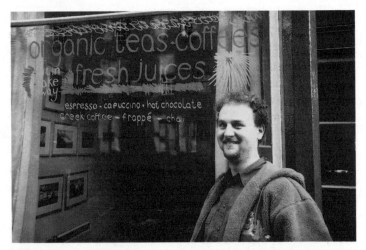

Nicolas outside the Lianachan café.

The Paper Chase

The problems start as soon as you decide on a name for your new business. Trading under your own name, or names if the business is a partnership, is relatively straightforward. However life can get complicated if you decide to trade under a separate business name.

Names that suggest a connection with the government, or which may be deemed offensive are non-starters. For example, the FART Bus Company in Spain would quickly offend the British sense of decency! Company's House has the complete list of trade names in use and can advise on any restricted words and phrases.

Then you have to let your local tax office know as soon as you start trading. The address is in the local telephone directory under "Inland Revenue". You also have to contact the local department of Social Security, who coordinates the payment of National Insurance.

You may also have to register to pay Value Added Tax although this depends on the business. Contact your local Value Added Tax Office, listed under "Customs and Excise" in the telephone directory, to find out if you do.

Limited companies have to be registered with the Companies House. They need to come up with the names of at least one shareholder, director, and company secretary, details of the share capital, a Memorandum of Association, and an Article of Association.

There are a host of other legal requirements in setting up a business. You may need a licence to carry out business activity from your local council or from national government departments such as the Department of Environment. This can apply to anything from pubs, hairdressers, dog breeders to sex shops. Nicolas' and Graham's café needed licences from the Department of Environmental Health to play music and prepare food. Selling alcohol and staying open late required separate licences.

It's best to contact a local Business Development Centre for advice on what applies to you. With all of Britain coming into line with European Union regulations, the rules and regulations are often being updated and reviewed.

If you are importing goods you'll need to contact the Department of Trade and Industry to get a licence and pay the relevant taxes. However it is worth asking your local Customs and Excise office for the tariff numbers of the goods you wish to import. Goods from the European Union come licence free and often without import tariffs.

Financing the Slippery Pole

Anyone who has set up a business knows how much initial investment is needed to get it up and running. That first lump sum of equity capital—usually twice as much as you initially expect—can make or break businesses as they struggle to get off the ground. There are all kinds of sources for funding in Scotland and most businesses draw on some combination of all of them.

Private Funding

Private funding is the obvious and most straightforward of options. This can be your own money and/or help from family and friends. The general rule is that if you can't put up around 30% of the start-up capital yourself, the banks won't show much interest in making up the shortfall.

Bigger businesses can also look for more formal help from Venture Capitalists, also known as "business angels." These "equity" investors look for their return in a share of the business profits and a cut of any sale. The money they give—generally over £300,000—is not expected to be repaid like a bank loan.

With such large sums involved, "business angels" will seldom look at anything other than established businesses with high profit turnovers that are looking to expand. If they do get involved they can bring with them a lot of kudos and expertise but they also expect have a significant say in how the business is run.

Public Sector

A softer option than fat cat "business angels" for new businesses is public sector funding. Government grants are generally more readily available in Scotland than in other European countries. Most sources of funding stress that the money must be used to fill in financial shortfalls instead of funding business start-up costs.

Big grants are more likely to go to employers who can promise work for more than 20 people. Manufacturing and high technology are the most favoured with retail and personal services raising little interest. The most important contact for grants between £50,000 and £500,000 is the Scottish Equity Partnership. Set up in 1996, the Partnership funds new and growing businesses. Several other grants are available for smaller businesses. However, these are often only advertised locally and are difficult to find. A good place to start looking is the Local Business Shop, a government information body offering information and advice on all business matters free of charge.

Nicolas is very grateful for the support that he got from the Edinburgh Small Business Gateway Service after deciding to set up his business. They helped him with an intensive course in how to set up and run a new business venture, follow-up support, and a small amount of cash to help get by in lean times.

"If we didn't have them we'd be lost in space," said Nicolas. "And they come free," he added.

Bank Loans

Banks generally provide no more than 40% of the financing for a new business venture. How successful you are with the bank depends on a number of factors. Most important is the quality of your business plan, the prospects for generating revenue over the medium term, and security for the bank.

"Security" is their guarantee that if it all goes pear-shaped and you have to close down, they can still get their original investment back. In other words, you may end up signing over your house as security for a loan.

Finding Business Premises

Buying a home is complicated enough in Scotland. There's an entirely new set of regulations that need consideration when buying or leasing a business property or running a business from home.

If you decide on setting up at home, then beware. The title deeds or lease of the property have to be free of restrictions as some prohibit business use on the premises. You also have to get the OK from the local Environmental Health Departments to check that you meet health and fire regulations. For example, if catering is involved, you will probably be required to have a separate kitchen, even if all you're making is tea and coffee.

You will also need to contact the planning department of the local council. If the business will mean an increase in traffic or noise, there is a good chance that complaining neighbours will force you to close shop. It's also a good idea to be sure that house insurance also covers business equipment, as many insurance companies are reluctant to take on the added risk.

If you are renting or buying a commercial property, the same system applies with finding a home. The best place to start looking is in the property pages of national and local newspapers. It's also worth being put on the mailing list of local solicitors, developers, surveyors, and estate agents as they also lease out and sell commercial property in Scotland. For small workshops or short-term rental, try Railtrack property (railway arches are a cheap way to start up), British Steel PLC and industrial estates found around most small towns.

The whole process can take a long time and be very expensive. Finding the right place for Nicolas' café took over a year. "We were looking for months, tramping the streets and wearing out our sandal leather," he said.

A small space of prime real estate in the centre of town didn't come cheap either. After forking out £4,500 worth of deposit money, Nicholas is committed to paying £2,500 every three months in rent for the next six years.

Get Yourself Connected

There are about 20 million new users logging onto the Internet every month. It's nothing short of a revolution in how we access and distribute information.

The business world has been quick on the uptake, recognising that e-commerce jumps the barriers of geography, time, and culture. You can buy almost anything online, from a pork pie to a private island. Many small start-up companies in Britain are making millions on the Internet, although the market is still volatile with fortunes made and lost in the blink of the stock market's eye.

Nowadays, technology means that most businesses can be run from home, all that is needed is a telephone, fax machine, and computer. This means that it is now possible for a person to live in a lovely Highland glen and still have his or her finger on the pulse of their business venture. Mobile phones and e-mail have made communication with the central workplace effortless. Buying the equipment is a simple affair. Office equipment, especially computers, is readily available from high street stores. Often the best deals can be found in computer magazines, available at most newsagents. Just make sure if you get one of these bargains that the guarantee is a good one.

Software can also be picked up from computer stores and is increasingly user friendly. If you are a novice to the computer world, the cheapest way of learning the ropes is through a do-it-yourself book that covers Information Technology (IT) in business. There are also courses available on the use of computers, from spreadsheets to desktop publishing. Courses that provide the best value are those run from adult education centres.

To set up an Internet and e-mail connection you need a computer with a modem, a phone line, and the relevant software. It is worth shopping around for the cheapest Internet Service Provider (ISP). The Internet is now widely available for just the cost of a local call. Internet cafés are also springing up across Scotland offering cheap Internet access together with the usual coffee and cake while you surf.

Businesses are now quick to get a presence on the Internet with their own web page. There are a plethora of design companies that will charge anything from a few hundred to thousands of pounds to put you on the net. Alternatively, designing your own page is relatively simple if you have the relevant software, some courage, and a little IT know-how. It's worth remembering that with approximately one website for every three people on the planet, designing your website so that it pops up on the main search engines is as important as having a site with all the bells and whistles.

Insurance

Getting the right insurance to cover potential disasters is essential in any business. There are a large number of insurance policies available that will cover premises, goods, and most eventualities.

If you employ people, you are obliged by law to take out employer's liability insurance. This protects you from accident or illness claims made by your employees. You can also get insurance to cover potential claims arising from faults in your products or from professional negligence.

If you need a vehicle for work it also needs business insurance. It's important to check that the insurance policy covers you and any employee using the vehicle for commercial activities.

It's best to shop around. You can either go straight to insurance companies or to an insurance broker; both are listed in the Yellow Pages. For the cost of a phone call and a small fee, insurance brokers will shop around the market for the cheapest quote and arrange for the relevant cover on your behalf.

Keeping Accounts

New companies, especially limited companies, generate mountains of paperwork. All invoices, receipts, and other papers should be kept on file, as it is necessary to have proof of all business transactions for the Inland Revenue or VAT inspectors. Accounts can and probably will be assessed by the Inland Revenue so it is important to be meticulous with bookkeeping.

Nicolas does his own accounts at Lianachan, a daily chore that involves logging in everything that he pays in and out of the business account. "This is for tax purposes," he tells me as he works on a sheet of finely scrawled figures. "But it is also useful for forecasts and budgeting." At the end of the financial year in April, his accountant tidies up and reviews the year's progress. A bigger business can, of course, afford to hand over everything to the accountant.

Either way, professional help from a lawyer or an accountant is essential, even if you can't afford the high fees. Lawyers are useful for drawing up a good business plan, applying for licences or for handling legal wrangles. Accountants help with annual accounts, Value Added Tax returns, and other financial matters.

It is important to estimate how much you are likely to have to pay and keep back enough money for the taxes when they are due. In

Britain, up to a year and a half can pass before a first demand is made for payment of a tax bill.

Survival

Back at the café, Nicolas eases back into his chair and looks out of the window with a weary smile. Although he's survived the process of setting up his own business, the stress and hard work is still far from over. He has to worry about advertising the café, cooking up novel and tasty dishes and paying the rent in a month's time.

But for the moment, he remembers the rewards of going it alone with a little help from his friends. "Being self-employed, that's what it is all about. It's worth it, it's an adventure. There's a lot of stress but we'll see it work out."

Chapter Six

ARTS AND ENTERTAINMENT

"Westering home, and a song in the air,
Light in the eye, and it's goodbye to care"

—Sir Hugh S. Roberton, Glaswegian conductor and
composer, *Westering Home*

There is much more to Scotland than mountains and lakes. The country also has a thriving arts and entertainment scene. Whether it be Edinburgh's crazy festival vibe, football, or a good old-fashioned ceilidh, Scotland is on a high right now. It seems that devolution has helped bring a cultural and political renaissance to the country.

MUSIC

It's Friday night and we are in the famous fiddler Dougie MacLean's pub, The MacLean's Real Music Bar, in the small Perthshire town of Dunkeld. The square room with a long L-shaped bar is shaping up for a big night, packed as it is with a mix of musicians, regulars, and the odd passerby like myself.

The din of conversation dies down as Dougie settles down at a table in the middle of the room with a group of players young and old. There are fiddlers, guitarists, a girl with a round drum bound with animal hide called a bodhran, and an old man with an accordion (or *squeeze box* as it is commonly called). They kick off the session with a slow tune and pick up pace as the evening goes on. Others come and go as they please, picking up the guitars that hang on the walls to pitch in for a tune or two before going back to their drinks.

At the end of the night the group plays the ferociously fast "Hangman's Reel." Everyone bursts into spontaneous applause before wandering out into the crisp autumn night. It's a familiar scene, repeated in bars up and down the country.

Folk music is alive and well in Scotland, particularly in the country. Most villages and towns in the Highlands have at least one local "ceilidh band" as they are known and the music is popular with young and old alike. The cities are no exception, just ask around to find out which are the folk pubs and turn up to see a folk jam, or session, as they are known in Ireland and Scotland alike. If you are lucky, you may see the tunes put to Gaelic songs. This is when the language truly comes into its own. The other option is to go to a ceilidh (see below) and dance to some of the reels yourself.

Bigger name bands advertise themselves in concert halls and clubs. Some bands such as Capercaillie, have such a large following that they tour Europe and beyond. Others fuse folk music with other styles, with varying results. I have heard Celtic folk music blended with rave music, African rhythms and salsa. Like all music, Scottish folk music is constantly changing and adapting to modern influences.

Scotland's musical talent isn't limited to folk music. There is also a thriving contemporary music scene in Glasgow. With live music venues such as the 13th Note, King Tut's Wah Wah Hut, The Garage, and Barrowlands, the city has plenty of space for up and coming bands to get themselves heard. As a result Glasgow boasts an impressive hall of fame over the past twenty years or so.

Scottish groups that have made names for themselves in Glasgow before hitting the big time include Hue and Cry, The Soup Dragons, Simple Minds, Texas, Del Amitri, and Wet Wet Wet. The latest Glaswegian group to find the limelight is Travis with their best-selling album *The Man Who*.

Edinburgh doesn't have the same pull for up-and-coming bands as Glasgow, mainly because it lacks the venues for them to play in. But it still boasts some success stories, such as the Bay City Rollers and more recently, Goodbye Mr MacKenzie and Finley Quaye.

DANCE

Just as Scotland has a vibrant folk scene, it maintains strong links to the past through the dancing of reels. No one really knows when reels date back to although it's thought they were around long before Christianity made it to the island.

Close to standing stones dating back 5,000 years in Orkney, they found carvings of chain figures not unlike the wheeling pairs of one of the most classic of dances, the foursome reel. What devilish combination of astronomy, worship, and flirtation the dances were then used for is a mystery.

In the 16th century, the dance's pagan past was found so suspect by God-faring Calvinists that they tried to ban them altogether. Scottish dancing went on regardless, becoming more and more sophisticated as it drew on similar traditions in France and the Basque country. None other than Mary Queen of Scots is credited with introducing some of the reels to the Scottish court from France in the late 16th century.

Once a ceremonial affair reserved for big occasions such as weddings, the dancing of reels is now a popular past time. The best way to take part is to look out for a ceilidh. "Ceilidh" is a Gaelic word, originally meaning "a meeting in a neighbour's house for a night of conversation, music, and storytelling." Nowadays it is a general knees-up to live folk music. You can find ceilidhs across Scotland throughout the year, although the season starts in earnest in late autumn and runs up until Christmas.

Many visitors that come to Scotland imagine ceilidhs to be very formal affairs, with participants dancing a series of set routines with measured precision. This couldn't be further from the truth. A ceilidh is a bawdy free for all where everybody drops their inhibitions and dances the night away with friends and strangers. The popular reels played at a ceilidh, such as the Eightsome reel, the Dashing White Sergeant, and Strip the Willow are easy to follow and the band usually takes dancers through the basic moves before setting out on each new tune. If you get it all wrong don't worry, it's all part of the fun.

Nothing beats a good ceilidh. For a start there are no age barriers and the crowd tends to be a mix of old and young alike. Kids, in particular, have a fantastic time. The atmosphere is very informal with none of the dress code or airs and graces of a Highland ball. The dancing matches the drinking—fast and furious. Before too long, the boys are asking all the girls up to dance to spin them off their feet, and everyone feels like friends. Right at the end everyone locks arms in a huge circle and sings an impassioned Auld Lang Syne before the final, reckless waltz.

The Highland balls, also held one night each year in the autumn are very different to ceilidhs. These are much more exclusive affairs, with long lines of tradition and etiquette. Most who go are from well-established families from the upper classes. Entry to outsiders is by invite only and there is a strict dress code of black tie or kilt for gentlemen and an evening dress for the ladies. If your attire is not up to scratch, you will be turned away at the door.

Dancing at the Highland balls is also much more formalised. The evening begins with a sit-down dinner, after which couples book dances with each other on dainty little cards. The reels themselves tend to be more complex, such as the Hamilton House and the Reel of the 51st and it's important to have some idea of what you are doing before taking to the floor. Despite all the added show, the spirit of a Highland ball is no different from that of a ceilidh—a magical occasion of dance and drink leaving you with tired legs and a soaring heart at the end of the night. The best known of the Highland balls are held in Oban, Skye, and Inverness.

Clubs

At the other end of the spectrum is that most modern of answers to traditional country dancing: club culture. There are plenty of different styles and venues to choose from in Scotland, ranging from the hyper cool dance clubs of Glasgow to downright tacky Madonna and Abba theme nights.

The rave culture with thumping techno music used to be a big part of the British scene. Although raves are not as popular as they used to be, the habit of taking drugs (such as ecstasy and speed) during raves hasn't, especially at high-energy dance nights.

Art

The art scene in Scotland is thriving at the moment. For the past decade, the art colleges in Glasgow, Dundee, and Edinburgh have drawn bright young talent from across Great Britain, making them cutting edge centres for contemporary painting, ceramics, and sculpture.

Painting has drawn high acclaim in Scotland ever since Scottish Colourists, often called "Glasgow Boys and Girls," painted landscapes, still-lifes, and portraits with bright, vivid brush strokes. The Glasgow Boys and Girls were Glasgow-based artists that brought fresh vigour and innovation in painting sculpture and decorative art between 1895 and 1920. Influenced by major movements of the time, such as Art

Nouveau, Impressionism, Cubism and Expressionism, they made Glasgow a European centre for the arts until the focus shifted to Paris in the 1920s. Painters such as James Paterson, James Guthrie, and James Nairn were known as the Colourists, for their bright and vivid style. A few of the better known Glasgow Girls are Jessie Newbury and Frances MacDonald.

Today, the craft of painting is still alive and well in Scotland, despite much of contemporary art moving into video installations and conceptual statements.

Visit the Modern Art Museum in Glasgow and you will see the works of some of the big names of the past decade, like Peter Howson, Jack Vettriano, and Ken Currie. Their big canvases explore darker impulses of intolerance and xenophobia, as well as modern secular religions such as football. John Bellany's watercolours and Jock McFadyen's sketches make up an eerie collection of portraits. Alison Watt and Jennifer Saville's portraits of women have also been very successful recently.

Sculpture in Scotland is no less exciting. A few names to look out for are Sir Eduardo Paolozzi's abstract pieces and, more recently, Kenny Hunter's work. Hunter's beautifully finished, life-sized plastic Christ can be seen at St Mungo's Museum of Religious Life and Art in Glasgow. It is also worth looking out for David Mach's Greek temples made out of tyres as well as Andy Goldsworthy's sublime workings of the natural environment.

The world of crafts is often overlooked in Britain, but is no less vibrant. In addition to native crafts such as basket weaving, there are strong glass and ceramic traditions in Scotland.

The big galleries in Edinburgh tend to draw the international art exhibitions. In recent years the National Gallery, Portrait Gallery, Modern Art Gallery, and Dean Gallery have held big retrospectives on the likes of Dali, Picasso, Klimt, and Cezanne. Since devolution, these galleries have also had the purchasing power to buy paintings by old masters such as Murillo, Botticelli, Guercino, and Canova.

THEATRE

Most people who know anything about the performance arts scene immediately think of the Edinburgh festival. This is hardly surprising as the three-week festival, running from the middle of August until the end of the first week of September, is the largest of its kind in Europe.

The atmosphere during the three weeks is electric. Edinburgh's population doubles in size as festivalgoers flock to the city from around the world. The cafés spill onto the streets and the streets themselves become a spectacle. Walk down the Royal Mile any time of the day and you'll encounter a heady mix of dance, street perform- ance, ticket touts in costume, hungover actors out of costume and a few fire jugglers to top it all off. That is of course, if you can see your way through the bustle of the crowds.

The Edinburgh festival is also a focal point for dance, literature, storytelling, comedy, and music, from all around the world. But for all the festival's pomp and spectacle, its roots are in the fringe. The festival's fringe consists of small-scale, low-budget theatre, per- formed by anyone who has something to say and wants to say it to an audience. Buy a festival guide and you are immediately struck by the myriad of differing venues in attics and basements across town, each one offering radical new drama. This is true democracy: anyone who wants to can become a performer, regardless of how good or bad they are.

Here are a few key pointers to surviving the three weeks of late summer madness with your sanity and bank balance intact:

• Find somewhere to stay early. All the bed and breakfasts and hotels are often fully booked weeks in advance. If you have friends in Edinburgh that you can stay with, get really friendly with them well in advance: even floor space is at a premium.

• Try and be there for the first week of the festival (the third week of August). The first few days are the freshest and most exciting. By the end of the three weeks the hectic atmosphere and cumulative hangovers have taken their toll on most festivalgoers.

Drumming up madness at the Edinburgh festival.

- Don't just go and see anything that catches your eye and don't believe anything ticket touts tell you. If they are to be believed, every show in town is earth-shatteringly brilliant, when in reality many are far from it. There are plenty of student productions with more enthusiasm than talent. Gone are the days when a show cost two or three pounds and you could try your luck with some obscure theatre and still have change left for a few drinks afterwards. Nowadays shows start at six or seven pounds, so it would be worth your while to do a little research. All the shows are extensively reviewed in the local and national newspapers, the official festival guide, and the events magazine. However, reviews can also be unreliable, and at the end of the day, nothing beats a recommendation from someone you know or meet who has seen the show.

- Once you know what you want to see, make sure you buy your tickets in advance. The most popular shows, particularly in the bigger venues, sell out well in advance.

- Think twice before you go to the Military Tattoo. The Military Tattoo, for many the highlight of the festival, has been running for over fifty years now. The event is a colourful spectacle of Scottish military parades and dance troops from all around the world. The whole evening, rounded off with an impressive display of fireworks, is a time warp back to the grandiose days of empire and imperial rule. Some tourists can't get enough of it but others come away wishing they had spent their money elsewhere.

- Remember that the festival is as much about the atmosphere and the street life as the shows. You are likely to see just as much sitting in a café and watching the world pass you by as paying to go to the theatre. All the bars and cafés are open for most of the night during the festival, so bring headache pills and don't expect to get much sleep.

By the last day of the festival in September, everything transforms. Summer ends abruptly, the visitors depart en masse, and the city's residents come out of hiding to reclaim the streets.

For all the post-festival sobriety, the world of theatre continues apace across Scotland. The bigger theatres tend to show less contemporary, more classical theatre. The audience is expected to be well turned out and to turn up on time. Many productions close their doors at the starting time, regardless of whether or not latecomers have tickets. The smaller venues host more experimental theatre productions and are much more informal.

LITERATURE

There is a rich literary tradition in Scotland, made all the richer by the diversity of expression available to native scribes. After all, where most writers have full command of one language, many Scottish writers have grown up with Scots, Gaelic, and English to choose from.

Celtic folk have also never been short of a story or two. Gaelic has always been an oral rather than a written language. So myths and legends were traditionally passed on from generation to generation in stories and especially in song. Old "waulking songs" as they are called, tell tales of men going off to the galleys, raids between the clans and of course stories of love found and lost. Many of these tales have made rich pickings for modern writers and the art of telling them orally lives on to this day.

Scottish literature tends to explore a number of interrelated themes. The following brief description of some of these themes should help send avid bookworms out on the long winding road of Scottish writing.

The Historical Novel

The historical novel was first developed during the second and third decades of the 19th century (known as the Scottish Enlightenment) by the likes of Sir Walter Scott. Since then, truthful historical settings have been blended with fictional characterisation to tell rich and informative tales.

Sir Walter Scott is undoubtedly the best known author of the Scottish Enlightenment. His epic novels, such as *The Heart of Midlothian,* are among the best examples of imagined characters rooted in historical fact. Although more renowned as a poet, James Hogg, a contemporary of Scott, explored the bloody aftermath of the Battle of Culloden in *Three Perils of Women.*

A number of historical novels were written in the last century, many of them touching on life in the Highlands before and after the clearances. Iain Crichton Smith's first novel *Consider the Lilies*, is a beautifully considered portrait of an old lady's last days in her croft before she was evicted by the Duke of Sutherland to make way for sheep. Louis Grassie Gibbon wrote a wonderful fictional trilogy of books, *Sun Set Song, Cloud Howe* and *Grey Granite,* about rural life in the northeast of Scotland. Of the three books, I think that *Sun Set Song* best captures a sense of the period and its landscape.

A Ripping Yarn

For a sea-faring people, stories of adventure and intrigue have always come easily. Many of the best remembered Scottish authors told "ripping yarns," high-spirited and fast-moving adventure stories that have kept their appeal through the ages.

The best known stories by Scottish authors have to be Robert Louis Stevenson's *Treasure Island* and Sir Arthur Conan Doyle's *Sherlock Holmes* novels. Compton Mackenzie's *Whisky Galore* is a classic fictional account of the disappearance of the shipwrecked SS *Politician*'s precious cargo in the island of Eriskay. *Whisky Galore* was made into a film of the same name and another of Mackenzie's novels, *The Monarch of the Glen,* has recently inspired a BBC television drama. John Buchan's adventures of Richard Hanney, (the man who knew too much) in *The Thirty Nine Steps,* also made it to the big screen, twice! In recent years, the *Harry Potter* series has been enormously successful, shooting its author J K Rowling to fame and fortune. The stories of one boy's fantastic adventures are meant for children but like all good children's books, are just as popular with grown ups. Isla Dewers' *Giving up Ordinary* and *It Could Happen to You* and Stella Duffy's *Immaculate Conceit* are light hearted, bawdy tales with strong female characters.

The Supernatural

It is hardly surprising that so many Scottish authors and poets would take an interest in metaphysical worlds beyond the one we can see and touch. Myths, fairies and other fancies have always been a part of Celtic people's imaginings.

Fictional encounters with the supernatural date back to before the mid 18th century. Robert Burns' comic masterpiece *Tam O'Shanter* tells of a dark encounter with witches on the road home from the pub. James Hogg's *The Private Memoirs and Confessions of a Justified Sinner* explores the supernatural and is considered by many to be the best Scottish novel to date. Robert Louis Stevenson's *Dr Jekyll and Mr Hyde* needs no introduction.

More recent literature that touches on mythic spaces includes Neil Gunn's superb *Highland River* and *The Green Isle of the Deep.* George Mackay Brown's poetry and novels are also sumptuously strange, such as his saga-like collection of poems *The Wreck of the Archangel.* Perhaps Alasdair Gray's *Lanark* also fits into this category, with his surreal evocation of a parallel city to Glasgow.

Social Realism

In recent times, authors have been keen to move away from old fables and the romance of bonnie Scotland of tartan and the bagpipes. Many have preferred to concentrate on the grimmer realities in Scotland of poverty, urban deprivation and frustrated, failed lives

James Kelman, recognised as one of the finest 20th century Scottish writers, was at the forefront of focusing on the modern urban reality. One of his best known novels, *A Chancer,* plots the decline of a compulsive gambler. Alan Spence's *Its Colours They are Fine* is

117

about the life and times of a Glasgow man . William McIlvanney's *The Big Man* is a tender portrayal of working class life in Glasgow. George Douglas Brown's *The House with the Green Shutters* is another excellent, if depressing read.

Tartan Noir

There has been a recent explosion of new Scottish writing much of it dark, humorous and violent. Much of this writing, known as tartan noir, is a kind of literary equivalent to the Quentin Tarentino film *Pulp Fiction,* only in a Scottish setting. It's a lost world of drugs, moral confusion and sudden death that reflects a very modern landscape.

The best known of this genre has to be Irvine Welsh's *Trainspotting,* an exploration into Edinburgh's underworld of drug addiction and poverty. *Trainspotting* is one of the few examples of cinema doing a novel justice. Glasgow writer Christopher Brookmyre's *The Country of the Blind* is another sassy venture into the darker sides of the human condition.

Iain Banks has become something of a phenomenon in the past few years. Since his explosive debut with *The Wasp Factory,* he has produced a stream of excellent novels at a consummate pace, many of them science fiction. I think his best to date are *Complicity* and *The Crow Road.* Ian Rankin, also writing under the pseudonym of Jack Harvey, has made a name for himself for his well crafted detective novels such as *Set in Darkness*.

Poetry

Poetry is impossible to pin down into a series of neat categories; it stands in the valley of its own making. Many of the authors mentioned above are or were poets and countless others have rhymed or sung their way into people's hearts. There is no point in attempting to list them all here but a few of the big names are Edwin Muir (also a novelist), Sorley Maclean, Norman MacCaig, Ian Chrichlan Smith, Edwin Morgan, and, of course, Robert Burns.

THE PRESS

Britain's national press has traditionally taken little real interest in Scotland. However since devolution the British papers have been quick to catch up, now producing Scottish editions to keep pace with the country's new political life.

The five London-based broad sheets that cover Britain daily are *The Guardian* (comfortably left), *The Times* and *The Telegraph* (predictably right), *The Independent* (tries to be true to its name) and *The Financial Times* (emphasis on Business). Of these, *The Financial Times* and *The Guardian* tend to have the best foreign news.

There is a big tradition across Britain of buying the Sunday papers on lazy Sunday mornings and pouring over them whilst drinking endless cups of tea. Most of the papers do big Sunday editions with travel sections for sun-soaked daydreaming. *The Observer* is one of Britain's oldest newspapers and only comes out on Sundays. In Scotland you can also choose from *Scotland on Sunday*, *The Sunday Herald* or the much loved *The Sunday Post*.

For a spicier slant than the erudite tones of broadsheets try one of the tabloid papers. These are the newspapers that dish the dirt; sex scandals, celebrity gossip and the other sensational stories. The Scottish versions of the British tabloids are *The Daily Star of Scotland*, *The Scottish Daily Mail*, *The Scottish Express*, *The Scottish Mirror* and *The Scottish Sun*.

Scottish news has long been covered in the country's two national publications, Glasgow-based *The Herald* and Edinburgh-based *The Scotsman*. Both are owned by the Scottish Media Group.

All the regions in Scotland are also well represented by local papers that mix local events with the bigger picture. For example Edinburgh has the *Edinburgh Evening News*, Glasgow the *Daily Record*. Aberdeen's *Press and Journal* is particularly good. It is also well worth looking out for the feisty little west coast paper, the *West Highland Free Press*.

Go to a magazine rack in a newsagent and pretty much everything on offer is produced outside of Scotland. In such a small country there just isn't the domestic market to publish a broad range of Scotland-specific material. One notable exception is the long running *Scottish Field,* a glossy magazine promoting country living for the stalking, shooting and fishing sect. There is also *Caledonia,* which covers mainly food and fashion, the more literary *Scots Magazine* and *Kitchen Bathroom and Bedroom Magazine* which speaks for itself.

For an alternative take on the mainstream news check out the *Big Issue,* sold by homeless people to help them make a living. Edinburgh's *Product Magazine,* available at arts centres, is also a good buy for a more artsy read.

Television

Britain prides itself on its high quality television. Old classics such as *Fawlty Towers*, *Dr Who*, and BBC documentaries are still broadcast across the world.

There are five main channels to choose from, screened across the British Isles. BBC 1 and 2 come without adverts. ITV, Channel 4 and Channel 5 have advertisements.

With the advent of new technologies there is now much more choice than before. Cable and digital television companies can hook you up to over 20 news programmes, sports and movie channels as well as online shopping facilities.

Scottish television is increasingly finding its feet in the age of devolution. The long established production company Grampian television continues to screen home grown material (much of it in Gaelic) in the North of Scotland. There is also a new Scottish TV cable channel, which screens some locally produced material as well as a lot of reruns and repeats.

Scottish news is well covered by a number of stations, most of them based in Glasgow. However exclusively Scottish BBC news is yet to come as the broadcasting rights remain in London.

Chapter Seven

FOOD AND DRINK

"Scots whisky is just about the only thing left that brings guaranteed and sustained comfort to mankind."
—Lord Boothby, Member of Parliament, in 1984

MEALS

The British Isles are not known for gourmet cuisine. In fact the native food is so unremarkable that rather than live on an eternal diet of "meat and two veg," the English have virtually adopted the Indian cuisine as their own.

121

It is therefore hardly surprising that the Scots are equally uninspired cooks. With limited sun in the summer and nine months of wind and rain in between, native produce has traditionally been a bit thin on the ground. Root crops such as potatoes, carrots, and swede have been plentiful since they were introduced in the 18th century, but fruit and vegetables more sensitive to the cold are largely imported from warmer climes. Native alternatives to the root crop are limited to apples, nuts, kelp from the sea and berries.

With so little to work with and the need for energy-rich carbohydrates to combat the cold, the Scots have never been big on delicate food. And who can blame them? With the wind whipping up a fury outside and icicles forming inside the kitchen, you can hardly imagine sitting down to a slice of melon, followed by chicken wrapped in asparagus with a hollandaise sauce. The Scottish tuck into wonders such as a fish supper (cod and chips), mince meat and potatoes (tatties'n' mince), blood sausage (known as black pudding), kippers, and the king of them all—the holy haggis.

Breakfast

The Scots don't shirk breakfast. The whole country tends to eat gargantuan breakfasts compared to much of continental Europe. The French or Italians settle for a coffee and a croissant in the mornings. Scotland is fuelled on bacon rolls, and that's just for starters.

The most traditional of breakfasts is, of course, porridge. This gloppy mixture of oats and water or milk can be delicious and sustaining. However, if badly prepared, it sticks to your gums and, when uneaten, turns as hard as concrete.

Porridge was a staple diet to generations of Scots. Traditionalists of the older generation will swear that the only way to eat it is just with water and a dash of salt. My father told me that it was standard practice for men going out "on the hill" to take a block of porridge that had been cooked until very thick, poured into a drawer, and allowed to harden. It was then cut into slices and was the main food for the day.

These days, eating porridge doesn't have to be such an earnest affair, in fact it can be very tasty indeed. Pinhead oatmeal, instead of rolled oats, soaked overnight and heated gently in a low oven is delicious. It is best mixed with anything from butter, cane sugar, cream, toasted almonds, fruit compote, to maple syrup or even whisky to give it a hint of the exotic.

For many, a bowl of porridge is merely preliminary to the main act—cue drums and the sound of sizzling fat—the cooked breakfast. People visiting the British Isles are generally astounded by their first encounter with a cooked breakfast, also known as an English or Scots breakfast. Certainly working through the mix of eggs, sausage, bacon, chips, mushrooms, toast, fried tomatoes, fried toast, and tea demands both perseverance and courage.

The Scottish version throws in a tattie scone, haggis, and black pudding (blood sausage is a more accurate description) for good measure. The principle is simple: Fry everything in oil or fat and eat it before it congeals to the plate. Even the tea usually comes with a thin greasy slick on top.

The tattie (potato) scone is a quintessentially Scottish invention, made all the more unusual by the fact that it looks more like a pancake than a scone. A good indication of the Scottish cuisine's traditional abhorrence of all things healthy can be found on the suggested meals on the back of one scone pack: "Top with baked beans or cheese or cover with scrambled eggs and bacon." Stodginess rules!

Cooked breakfasts are most commonly found in small cafés, often called "greasy spoons." Usually workman's cafés, these scruffy no-fuss institutions pour out an endless stream of fried food and gallons of stewed tea. The pictures on their walls of faded pastoral scenes contrast with the harsh scrape of stainless steel cutlery on china, cigarettes drawn through yellowed fingers, and the low drone of conversation. There is something both comforting and vaguely depressing about these places where time stands still, and few bother to take off their coats.

Hairy steak: a Highland cow makes for a tasty morsel.

Scottish breakfasts are also the standard fare of most hotels and bed and breakfasts. You are more likely to experience the top end of the market, such as a plate of smoked salmon and scrambled eggs, together with bacon, sausage, black pudding, haggis, and a tattie scone.

Those who can't afford smoked salmon substitute it with smoked herring or kipper. This tastes best when grilled or poached in milk and eaten with a fried egg. Although delicious, smoked herring, most famously made in Arbroath and known as "Arbroath smokies," are guaranteed to stink up the kitchen for days!

Lunch

This can be a meagre affair if you're already carrying around the best part of Noah's Ark in your stomach. Lunches, particularly in cities and towns, tend to be taken quickly or on the hop. The exception is Sunday lunch when many families sit down for a roast, usually lamb or beef, two boiled vegetables, and roast potatoes with gravy.

Walking past a High Street baker between 12:00 pm and 2:00 pm will give you some idea of the typical Scottish lunchtime diet. School children and adults queue onto the streets for their rolls, pies, pasties, crisps, and donuts. Scotland has a very sweet tooth. Sweets and chocolates are consumed nonstop by children. Every newsagent, general store and gas station has them laid out in racks like glittering jewels. My dentist once told me that she has to frequently fill holes in children's first set of teeth, let alone the second lot.

Tea

Tea at 11:00 am, known as elevenses, mid-afternoon tea at 4:00 pm, and high tea at 6:00 pm are now a fading tradition. The demands of living and working in a modern world have largely put paid to these quiet moments in urban centres. In the country and in particular among the older generation however, teatime still holds sway as a daily ritual in the home.

There is nothing more comforting than sitting with friends or family around a table carefully laid out with pots of tea and a collection of cakes and scones. My great-aunt Kat is a master at the British variation on the tea ceremony. Now in her nineties, she still won't entertain any help, chatting away as she busies herself with pots of tea and scones pulled straight from the oven to be smothered with butter, homemade jam, and heather honey.

She sits me down and pours the tea from a huge pot with her ancient hands. She is so petite these days that the teapot seems to dwarf her and she practically uses her whole body weight to counter lever the pouring tea.

Scones—plain or with cheese or raisins—are only a part of the traditional spread. There is also shortbread (made from butter and flour), oatcakes, and Scottish pancakes. The pancakes are laden with butter and jam or honey. Cakes come in all shapes and sizes but is generally make with dried fruit. The best known is the Dundee cake, a sweet malty loaf crammed with fruits.

In recent years, the importance of tea as a national cure-all waned a little with the arrival of good coffee. Up until recently, the only coffee you could find outside of home was ropy old filter coffee in a teacup. Nowadays, you can find a decent cappuccino in most cafés. Café culture in the cities has taken over from the more formalised tradition of afternoon and high tea.

But a nice cup of tea—generally milky and without sugar—still holds a certain mystique in Scotland and Britain in general. It oils the wheels of social interactions, work breaks, and provides comfort in times of crisis. It even defines you to some extent; the working classes go for the strongest blends with lots of tannin and sugar, middle-class folk drink the exotic and aromatic varieties such as Lapsang Souchong and Earl Grey, and alternative types settle for herbal teas made from roots, flowers, and bark.

Dinner

Dinner, also known as supper or sometimes as tea, is the most important meal of the day. It is generally served between 6:30 pm and 8:00 pm, remarkably early compared to Italian or Spanish standards. It's the great coming together of families, lovers, and friends, when differences are laid aside or lain open again around the table.

What is on the table varies immensely, but Scotland offers an impressive array of native game and fish to choose from. Most famous is venison, or deer. Available all year round at no small expense, venison has a strong, distinctive flavour and is best roasted slowly with fresh berries such as juniper and blaeberries—also wild and native to the area. It is also wonderful in a casserole with a lot of red wine added to the pot.

There's plenty more wild game to choose from, such as hare, rabbit, partridge, pheasant, grouse, duck, and pigeon. Wild game is tougher than the average chicken or lamb and is best marinated and cooked slowly. These days game is rarely seen on the table. High prices, conservation concerns, and the takeover of supermarket shopping has made such food increasingly the domain of exclusive restaurants.

Not so for the fruits of the sea. Being a part of the British Isles and surrounded by so many deep oceans, fish still makes up an important part of the diet. A good fishmonger in Scotland bristles with choice: oyster, muscle, crab, squat lobster, prawn, whitefish, herring, cod, flatties, monkfish, halibut, skate, mackerel, and John Dory stare out from plastic trays at passers by.

Most traditional of all is the herring. The herring once sustained thousands of fishermen up and down the coastlines. It's said that long before the toll bridge was built over to the island of Skye, you could walk over from the mainland hopping from small fishing boat to boat.

Herring was also a staple food for poor folk, smoked, salted, or pickled to keep it longer. Salted herring would be soaked overnight, hung, and grilled to make Buft herring or "bufters," the 19th century version of deep fried cod. A classic Scots folk song praises the strength and bravery of Scots men before coming up with the explanation: "For the lads have been fed upon tatties and herring". Herring catches have long since been exhausted and even cod, the modern-day alternative, is becoming increasingly expensive as numbers dwindle.

Although fantastically fresh seafood, not to mention trout and salmon from the rivers, is still readily available in Scotland, the Scots aren't very inventive when it comes to preparation. Everything is generally fried in batter or grilled with butter and lemon. Fresh fish prepared simply is often the best: A small "breakfast" trout—caught the same morning—rolled in oats and fried with butter settles any debate.

Tastes and culinary practices are also changing. Seafood cafés and restaurants now produce well-thought-out and prepared dishes. The best plate of mussels I've had in my life, cooked with herbs and white wine, was in a tiny café on the island of Mull.

Haggis'n Clapshot

Haggis with tatties (potatoes) and neeps (turnips) come closest to being Scotland's national dish. It's certainly the first thing that comes to mind when one thinks of Scottish food, although this could have something to do with the memory of how long it lingered in the stomach the last time it was eaten. Dreamt up in a distant past when times were hard and livestock eaten down to the very marrow in their bones, the haggis is a creative way of using up what's left when the prime cuts are finished.

In short, it is offal, heavily disguised with oats, spices, and pepper, but still offal. What it lacks in content it doesn't exactly make up for in presentation either. The whole meal is blended and stuffed into a sheep's stomach to be baked or boiled and served up with more boiled tatties and neeps. You have to hand it to the Scots for coming up with the concept of the haggis as a national dish.

You can buy haggis from the local butcher and delicatessen or make it yourself. The following recipe demystifies the haggis down to its constituent parts, served in a bowl rather than the old sheep's stomach.

Makes two large haggises, each serving six:

<u>Ingredients</u>

Sheep's or ox's heart, without fat or tubes	0.5 kg/1 lb
Sheep's or ox's liver	0.5 kg/1 lb
Stewing steak, without fat	0.2 kg/0.5 lb
Shredded or finely minced suet	113 g/ 4 oz
Large onion, grated	2
Salt	2 teaspoon (tsp)
Freshly ground black pepper	0.5 tsp
Coarse oatmeal	0.2 kg/0.5 lb

Blend all ingredients well. Lightly press into two well-greased (preferably with some form of animal lard) 1 litre/ 1 quart bowls. Cover with foil. Steam in a huge pan for 3 hours. The simmering water should come halfway up the bowls and be replenished if and when the level drops. Serve with "bashed neeps and tatties" (well-mashed turnips and potatoes). A good thick beef or lamb gravy also goes well with haggis.

As awful as it all sounds, a haggis is surprisingly tasty on a chilly night with a tot of whisky over it. Another way to eat it is to slice it, and fry it in butter until crisp.

The modern-day haggis has been forced to accommodate a growing population of vegetarians in Scotland. Vegetarian or "white haggis" is now a widely popular alternative to the old blood and guts version. However the thought of introducing vegetables to the haggis concept, let alone excluding meat all together, is still unacceptable to some old traditionalists. One friend, Marcus Noble, took a white haggis back to his grandfather one Sunday, only to be virtually thrown out of the house along with the vegetarian offering. "Vegetarian haggis. How could you go that way?" his grandfather bellowed.

One thing to look out for if you're a newcomer to Scotland is the standard joke about where "the wild hairy haggis" is from. Reader beware! Haggises are not elusive Highland animals that live in the hills and have to be hunted and skinned for the table. Given half a chance many Scots will reel out a complex description of the haggis' feeding habits and mating patterns before letting the perplexed visitor in on the joke.

The Gravy Train

A nice plump haggis is more a symbol of a uniquely Scottish food invention than something that is eaten daily by the population. These days the Scots go for more generically British fare when it comes to the national pastime of eating heavy foods.

Chips, thick-cut and greasy, are a standard compliment to a few beers. Bought from a late night "chippie" or chip shop, customers order their chips and choose a fish or meat product from a selection of objects laid out behind a brightly-lit glass-fronted counter. Their choice, generally a slice of cod or sausage is dipped in a mixture of flour and water and then deep-fried in oil. The whole lot, chips and all, are wrapped in paper to be wolfed down with fingers on the street.

The Scots, creative in all aspects of life, have added to the usually limited chip-shop fare in their own inimitable style. There is the Scotch pie, bits of generic meat in gravy encased with crusty pastry, or the macaroni cheese pie for vegetarians. You can also wash down a few beers with a mini haggis deep-fried in batter or an obscenely large pink sausage.

Two Glaswegian inventions, deep-fried battered pizza and—wait for it—a battered chocolate or "Mars" bar have been all the rage in the last few years. The "Mars" bar is a little harder to find these days in an average chippie, but can be made up on the pleading request that you've never tried it before. Friends that have tried it have told me that it may wreck your waistline but is a small price to pay for a little slice of heaven.

After making a soggy selection from a Scottish chippie you may be asked "Salt 'n sauce?" (Most common in Edinburgh). This means: "Do you want salt and a thick brown liquid with a burnt barbecue taste over your greasy chips?" The man or woman behind that high chippie counter may as well be asking, "Would you like a premature heart attack from cholesterol overdose with your meal?" It's no wonder that Glasgow, the home of the battered pizza, also has the highest rates of heart disease in the Western world.

Doughnut Heaven

Glasgow is no exception when it comes to diet-related illnesses in Scotland. Stodgy food and lack of exercise puts Britain at the top of the coronary heart disease table in Europe. According to the British Heart foundation, amongst European Community countries, only Ireland and Finland have a higher rate of heart attacks than Britain.

Ask any doctor in Scotland and they will tell you that the young don't eat enough fruit and vegetables and they drink and smoke too much when adults. The diets of the elderly aren't much better either.

I remember coming across a nurse who was cleaning out an old pensioner's house who had died the week before. She was pushing a wheelbarrow piled high with cans of tinned rice pudding, half of them long out of date. Apparently that's all he ate.

One eminent professor of preventative cardiovascular medicine at the Imperial College London, Neil Poulter, summed up the nation's predicament in the *Guardian* newspaper:

"We've got high levels of smoking, we've got a high fat intake, cholesterol levels are up and we're overweight. We've got high blood pressure and we have too much salt in our diet. And we don't exercise. More than 30% of the population do nothing whatsoever apart from breathing. And it's getting worse."

That great British staple, the cooked breakfast is blamed for "killing more people than the British army."

There is a growing shift in awareness of the importance of healthy eating amongst those who can afford it. Organic foods, produced without any pesticides or artificial fertilisers are increasingly the rage. In addition to food shops offering fresh organic fruit and vegetables, all of the main supermarkets have responded to consumer demand by turning large sections of their shelves over to organic produce. It's now becoming much easier to find fresh and affordable organic produce in Scotland.

Concern over food isn't only limited to the potential damage from eating too many pesticides. A series of food scares in recent years has made the public very aware of just what it is they are eating. The scare over bovine spongiform encephalopathy (BSE) or mad cow disease as it is more popularly known, has had the greatest impact. In the 1980s, farmers fed cows with a feed that contained organic parts of slaughtered sheep, and feeding it to cows to keep costs down. Unfortunately the cows ended up with a form of scrapie, a fatal brain disease in sheep that turned the cows into pseudo-carnivores and led to BSE.

Further up the food chain, man eats mad cow and ends up with a similar disease years later. Doctors are waiting with baited breath to see whether eating infected beef in the late 1980s and early 1990s is going to produce a time-delayed epidemic in humans in years to come. Scots aren't too worried however, as Scottish cows were largely unaffected by mad cow disease.

The advent of genetically modified crops on the scene has understandably inflamed an already jittery public. Selected test sites across Britain have been growing genetically modified crops since 1998. Although mass production has been ruled out, many believe that the growth of the industry and genetically modified crops will mushroom out of control before we can be sure that they won't be harmful to humans. Protestors have gone as far as destroying test sites, often with broad public support, and many supermarkets will not stock genetically modified products.

Pudding
If all this isn't enough to give you indigestion, there is still dessert, or pudding, as it's commonly known. No proper sit-down meal in Scotland is complete without a sweet pudding.

What desserts in Scotland may lack in finesse, they more than make up for by being rich, yummy, and filling. Nothing comes close to the taste of a good crumble, usually eaten hot and topped with cream, ice cream, or custard. A crumble is made from whichever fresh fruit is in season, such as rhubarb, apple, gooseberry or damson, and then oven-baked with a crispy flour and butter topping.

There are plenty more sweet winter warmers that deserve a mention but in the end words alone won't do them justice. It's best if you can sample the taste of bread pudding or a jam roly-poly yourself. One old favourite is easy to make whether you're in Scotland or abroad. It is a Highland dish called *cranachan*, also called *cream crowdie*, served on special occasions. Note that my recipe calls for heather honey. Although this is not an essential ingredient, it tastes superb regardless of what it's poured into or spread onto.

Ingredients

Double cream	0.3 litres/0.3 quarts
Toasted oatmeal	4 tablespoons (tbsp)
Whisky or Drambuie	3 tbsp
Heather honey	3 tbsp

Toast the oatmeal in the oven until crisp and lightly browned. Sweeten the cream to taste with heather honey. Whip the cream and whisky until it is thick, then fold the oatmeal into the cream and serve cool but not chilly.

What relatively limited fresh native fruits there are in Scotland are made good use of. Autumn in the Highlands is a time to fill the larder with an impressive array of jams, pickles and chutneys, to preserve a taste of summer's fruits long into winter. I remember as a child, being sent out in September with friends to pick blackberries or blueberries only to come back with black mouths smeared with dark juice and a meagre half tub of fruit for making jam.

EAT, DRINK, AND BE MERRY

Gone are the dark days when there were few options outside of chips, or maybe a pizza in most Scottish towns. There are an increasing number of restaurants offering international foods as varied as Chinese, Mongolian, and Malaysian. Italian, Indian, and kebab cafés tend to be the most prolific. Most restaurants have a vegetarian menu and some are entirely turned over to non-meat eating.

Tipping varies from place to place. Some include an obligatory 10%, clearly marked on the bill at the end of the meal. However most rely on the discretion of the customers and 10% of the price of the meal is considered acceptable. Catering staff are notoriously underpaid and poorly treated in Scotland, so tips are always very welcome. Most restaurants stop serving at 9:00 pm and some keep their kitchens open until 10:00 pm, but seldom any later.

Food Shopping

Supermarkets and busy urban lives mean that people tend to put less time into cooking well-thought-out meals with local ingredients. The popularity of the vast selection of packaged meals available in most supermarkets is evidence enough that the same care and time isn't put into cooking these days.

Supermarkets that set up shop on the outskirts of the towns draw trade away from small local outlets. The local butcher and fruit and vegetable shops have had to contend with cheaper and more convenient shopping in the big supermarkets. But in more isolated country areas the general store is still the local community's lifeline. Often housing the post office as well as provisions and newspapers, the village shop is the focal point of both trade and gossip.

Whisky

No other spirit is so intimately connected to the spirit of a nation. After all, a bottle of whisky is—with the exception of men in skirts—the first thing that comes to mind when one thinks of Scotland. It is also the nation's primary earner, providing a big boost in exports to the British economy as a whole. It's not surprising that old, limited edition bottles can go for up to £2,000 a throw.

Despite some of the crazy prices on some bottles of malt whisky, its mystique is far more than just clever marketing. It is, after all, made up from Scotland's primal elements—barley from the earth, water from the rivers and streams, fire to malt the yeast and the damp, pure Highland air that matures the whisky through heavy oak casks.

Moreover the mystery of its creation is uniquely Scottish. No other country in the world that has attempted to use the same ingredients and techniques to distil their own whisky has come anywhere near to the taste and quality of Scottish whisky. The Spanish, Germans, Americans and Japanese have all tried with limited degrees of success. But then much of a whisky is in its obscure Gaelic names such as Balvenie, Lagavulin or Laphroaig, so often mispronounced by visiting tourists. The Spanish imitation, called Dick whisky, hardly swings it. Only the Irish, so close in geography and spirit to Scotland, can match Scottish whisky in quality.

Many Scots say the magic that makes their whisky better than anyone else's is in the water from their Highland rivers. Although there is no evidence to support this, the word for whisky itself has root in the old Gaelic term for water, *uisge*. *Uisge beatha*, meaning *the water of life*, is the Gaelic term for whicky. Perhaps there is something to the praise muttered between sips, "Ah, 'tis the water of life."

It is thought that Saint Patrick from Southern Scotland brought the early knowledge of whisky distilling from Ireland around the mid-5th century A.D. Knowing they were on to a good thing, the art of whisky production was kept a closely guarded secret by the early Christian monastic community right into the 15th century when the first written record pops up of its use for "medicinal purposes." From then on whisky became a domestic affair with most Scottish homes brewing their own versions.

It wasn't until the 1840s that whisky's potential as a big earner was realised and big distilleries were built to produce it on a grand scale. They never looked back. Today whisky is one of the top five UK export earners, competing with cars, aircraft, oil and the computer industry on the export market. If you buy a £12 pound bottle of whisky in Britain, around £8 pounds of that goes to the taxman. It's said that all the gold bullion in London doesn't add up in value to the whisky reserves in Scotland. Better still, whisky directly employs 14,000 people north of the border, with a further 47,000 people involved indirectly in the industry.

Malts versus Blended

Whisky is a good thing all round for the Scots, but drinking it is not without its pitfalls for the uninitiated. To start with, there are whiskies and there are *whiskies*. Much is made of the difference between a standard blended whisky—or scotch—and it's finer cousin, the fine single malt.

The blended whiskies, which make up most of the exports, are standardised by being mixed together to produce a cheaper and more predictable result. The single malts are produced from one distillery and matured for a minimum of 10 years in oak casks. The difference in quality, and price, between a single and a blended whisky is put down to the distinctive flavour of each malt that comes from the particular water and air of each distillery.

Whether you drink a blended or single malt depends on the occasion. The good blended whiskies, such as Bell's and Famous Grouse are the work horses that oil the cogs of daily living in Scotland. These blends make up the standard fare in pubs, often drunk neat with a beer—this is known as a "chaser"—or mixed with coca-cola or with ginger wine—a "whisky Mac."

A bottle of blended whisky, or "the creature" as my Scottish uncle used to call it, sits in a cupboard in most Scottish homes to be dipped into on a cold night or when friends or family are around.

The versatile whisky even doubles up as medicine for mild ailments. Mixed with hot water, honey, and lemon (known as a hot toddy) it is used as a cure-all from colds and flu to a warmer after a long day out on the hill. It may also be rubbed neat on baby's gums to deaden the pain from new teeth coming through, as well as giving them a lifelong taste for the milk of the motherland.

It is also seen by many as an essential tonic to ease the pains of old age. Ninety-nine-year-old Lord Shinwell suggested introducing whisky into the House of Lords, that domain for ageing aristocracy, as a legitimate expense with the claim that, "...many of them cannot do without it because it is in the nature of a medicine." Shinwell also tried, and failed, to make blended whisky available on the National Health Service.

The malt whiskies, on the other hand, have an air of the sacred about them, although this can often have more to do with clever marketing than the quality of the drink itself. Even the most discerning of wine producers are unlikely to go as far as describing their product as having: "The aroma of diesel oil and tar, seaweed and iodine, fishing net and fishing boats," as Laphroaig whiskey claimed in an advertisement.

Stored in their tall cylinder boxes for months on end, malts are usually opened only on special occasions and even then just for a taster, or a "wee dram." Malt is typically the centrepiece of a toast. It is brought out to celebrate occasions such as the birth of a newborn baby, the parting of friends, or the sealing of a business deal. Bringing out the malt is a ceremonious affair. It should never be asked for, only offered by the host.

Contrary to common perception, most Scots don't say, "a wee dram for the road," these days, having seen fellow countrymen doing it too often in films over the years. The term "dram" has fallen out of favour now, and people prefer to measure their firewater in singles or doubles. The equivalent measurement for a dram is an old quarter gill, or in modern terms, a double.

A malt whisky should only be drunk out of a whisky glass and is never mixed with anything but pure water. Ice is definitely not allowed. So much as waving a bottle of coke near single malt will drain the blood from most Scots' faces. There are some that say that even adding water to a malt whisky is tantamount to sacrilege. But a little extra water—especially Highland water—has never done a whisky any harm, in fact it can often help to release the flavours.

Much has been written about malt whisky's differing flavours or "characters." The clearest distinction that can be made is between the mainland and island malts. The peaty water used in the islands is mixed with seaweed, bringing with it a more pungent and smoky character. Try one of the Isle of Jura malts, famed for their distinctive flavour.

In truth, much of the reams of literature on the back of whisky bottles is a fanciful mixture of hocus pocus and snobbery. Of course whisky does vary widely from region to region and from distillery to distillery. But in the end it all comes down to personal taste. When attempting to choose from the dazzling choice of different brands and blends, it's best to remember the old Scottish adage: there is no such thing as bad whisky, just good whisky and better whisky.

Bacardi and Tizer

Distinctly Scottish brews don't stop with whisky. As well as a number of Scottish beers and ales, such as McEwans and Tenants, the country has its own unique soft drinks, Irn Bru and Tizer. Someone told me that Scotland is the only county in the world where Coca Cola isn't the most popular national soft drink because the Scots prefer Irn Bru.

Both drinks' mix of glucose, flavourings, orange colouring, and fizz is not for the fainthearted. Kids tend to get a taste for it young and there's a free bottle of Tizer in some old bars to add to beer or whisky. In one of Billy Connolly's best gags, that most famous of Scottish comedians wakes up in the morning in his bathroom with one of the worst hangovers of his life after a heavy night drinking and laments, "Never again, Baccardi and Tizer!"

Irn Bru in particular holds a real soft spot in this nation's sentimental heart. There is something timelessly Scottish, and in particular Glaswegian, about a bottle of Bru. It's especially essential to the tradesman reading a copy of the *Daily Record* on a building site—his bum hanging out of his pants, a cigarette smoked down to the filter, and a bottle of Irn Bru for company.

Chapter Eight

THE GREAT OUTDOORS

"Always had a roof above me, always paid the rent and I've never set foot in a tent. I couldn't build a fire to save my life, I lied about being the outdoor type…God bless the great indoors."

—Lyrics from *The Outdoor Type* by Lemonheads.

A low slanting October sun floods into the glen. It lights up the countryside like it's one of those romantic last scenes of a movie where the hero strides off into a brightly painted sunset. The bracken is lit a rusty orange, the grass seems to be on fire, the birch trees shimmer with greens and yellows, and the berries on the rowan trees are a deep glowing red. The sky beyond is black with rain and a passing rainbow showers down curtains of colour, as if there weren't enough already. We walk on knowing that every bend on the winding track out of Glen Affric will bring fresh wonders.

In a world increasingly choked with traffic, noise, and pollution, much of Scotland offers a wonderful contrast. It has rainbows, clean running rivers, space to breathe, and a magical silence. There is something of every northern country about the thin light and water-rich lands but Scotland is unique, holding a timeless mystery. No other countryside I've seen has touched me in quite the same way.

It is not surprising that the country has become such a haven for outdoor types. Most settle for hillwalking, ranging from short easy treks to the restless search for windswept mountain peaks. Walking alone is not always enough. The Scots have also found all kinds of ways of entertaining themselves while they walk through the country-side. Hitting a small ball with a stick and shooting or stalking wild game comes immediately to mind.

But there is more. "Scotland offers unlimited options for leisure," touts one local guide book. So then, just what are all these leisure options and are they really unlimited?

ON THE ROAD

The first and least taxing way of enjoying the great outdoors is from the safety and comfort of the car or caravan. In this age of mobile living, many take to the open roads with their seatbelts firmly attached. Britain becomes caravan country in the summer, when the older and more sedate take their homes with them and drive, tortoise-like, from caravan park to caravan park. Caravan culture is a modest and private affair where strangers park in neatly packed terrace formation in a caravan park, sometimes only to stay bunkered in their bubble homes pointedly ignoring their neighbours.

The less fortunate in the automobile world who can't afford caravans take day trips in their cars to park at roadsides, eat sandwiches, drink flasks of tea and admire the countryside, sometimes even with the windows rolled up. It may be a surprise if you are new to Scotland and you stop in a car park in the country to find half of the cars occupied with the windows steamed up. Don't worry, they're just drinking tea and that's normal here.

HILLWALKING AND CLIMBING

Hillwalking or climbing can be physically demanding but travelling through Scotland's wide-open spaces on foot is definitely well worth the blisters. In many ways, this simplest of outdoor pursuits in Scotland is also one of the most satisfying. No other means of travel gives you the time to soak in and appreciate the beauty of your natural surroundings.

Much of this popularity is due to the unprecedented freedom of access walkers in Scotland enjoy. Unlike England, which has strict trespassing laws, Scotland is wide open to walkers and climbers alike. You can pretty well chart your own route through the glens and to the top of the mountain of your choice.

The only exception is during the deerstalking season when walkers can scare off the prey and put their own lives at risk from stray bullets. If you are setting out for anywhere high and wild from September through November, call the local estate to see if they are stalking. Sundays are rest days for stalkers and deer alike.

Climbing mountains in Scotland is often called "walking the hills." Don't be confused into thinking that these are gentle ambles, they are real mountains and real challenges. Walking the hills in Scotland has its own terminology. People don't walk or climb up mountains in Scotland, they "bag Munros." A Munro refers to a mountain with a height of over 3,000 feet. Munros are named after Sir Hugh Munro who famously charted the hundreds of high peaks in Scotland in the early part of the 20th century.

To "bag" a Munro, you have to climb it and touch the pile of stones, or cairn, at the top before moving swiftly onto the next one. Some turn this practice into a kind of personal trial, seeing how many Munros they can bag in a summer.

Calling a mountain a "Munro" isn't the only source of confusion when it comes to navigating your way across Scotland on foot. Gaelic names for hills, lakes, streams, and more besides add to the Scottish landscape's distinctive romance. The very sound of the valleys and villages conjures up a lyrical charm: Kinlochleiven, Achlachan moss, Rubha Ruadh.

For those who wish to set a more leisurely course to a mountain top, there are countless well-marked nature trails across Scotland that cater for both day-trippers and hardcore backpackers. Most famous of these are the Southern Upland Way and the West Highland Way. The Southern Upland Way runs 341 km (212 miles) from the west coast in Portpatrick to the Cockburnspath on the Berickshire coast south of Dunbar. The West Highland Way starts in Milnagavie just North of Glasgow and finishes up some 95 miles (152.9 km) North in Fort William. Many finish off the Highland walk by walking up Scotland's highest peak, Ben Nevis, which looms out of the spectacular scenery of Glen Coe. Leaflets of outings, walks, and trails are available from local tourist information centres.

Many come to see the wild life that inhabits this land of mountain, sea, and rainbows. Bird watchers, with their array of binoculars and bird identification books are in paradise. There is nothing more arresting than a glimpse of majestic golden eagles making lazy circles high in a mountain pass. There are reportedly only 160 nesting pairs left in Scotland. Rarer still is the capercaillie, an elusive woodland bird with a shrill, distinctive call. Few ever see a capercaillie, which now faces extinction due to growing pressure on its woodland habitat.

Scotland is also a popular destination for migratory birds, especially feathered escapees from winters in Iceland and Greenland. Look out for ducks, coots, geese, rare swans such as the mute and whooper, waders, grebes, oyster catchers, and ringed plovers. For novice "birdies" like myself, nothing beats the long call of oyster-catchers as they lift gracefully off the incoming wash of a sandy beach with a flash of orange beaks.

Land and sea mammals are also abundant. Many of the beasts still found in the wilds of Northern Scandinavia, such as wolves, bears, and wild boars, have long since disappeared. However foxes, hairy mountain goats, and deer still stalk the land. Along the coasts there are colonies of seals with their big watchful eyes and a few extremely shy sea otters. Marine tourism is also on the rise. Tour operators offer trips to see dolphins, porpoises, puffin colonies, and minkie whales.

Scotland isn't a leisure park and exploring it can be risky. Much of the country is wild and barren and every year walkers and climbers lose their way down ravines or off cliffs. Most notorious is Ben Nevis, Scotland's highest mountain. In the winter the routes up are treacherous. I remember reading in one particularly cold winter how 15 people hadn't made it off the "hill" alive. Just outside Tyndrum in the Central Highlands, a roadside cairn is dedicated to the hundreds of walkers who have died in the Cairngorm Mountains in the last century. The cairn, built from stones taken from the tops of over four hundred surrounding mountains reads, "They died in a place they loved."

The Mountain Rescue Service in Scotland is famed for the lives it saves every year. Too many people get into trouble because they aren't well prepared. The trick is to be ready for every eventuality. As well as the regular hillwalker's clobber such as good boots and a tent, you need waterproofs from head to foot, shorts, sunglasses, sunscreen, warm clothing, windproof hats, and scarves. A day out can feel like a constant striptease as you juggle the layers between hot, wet, and biting cold.

I remember walking up a hill by Loch Hourn on the west coast one unexpectedly warm September day. It was a bright autumn day and the view was fantastic. Not that it made much impression on us as we trudged up the path weighed down by several layers of clothes—

thermal underwear, two jumpers, a wind stopper and a heavy water-proof. I felt like a human boiler, letting off puffs of steam like some overheated cartoon character.

When we reached the top of the hill everything about the weather changed in an instant, clouding over and pouring down first rain, then sleet, then snow. With visibility down to a just few feet, we crouched by a big stone for protection, disorientated and assailed by the elements. In a country of sudden contrasts, foul weather can regularly gatecrash on a sunny day only to evaporate just as quickly as it appeared.

Good orienteering skills are just as important as equipment. A map and compass are essential for long walks that don't follow well-marked paths. Ordnance Survey, or OS maps as they are commonly called, are available in most bookshops and tourist offices. They provide detailed and extensive coverage of Scotland's every nook and cranny.

When setting out hillwalking, it's best to keep in mind the following safeguards:

• Check the weather reports. Forecasting the weather, which can change rapidly, is a notoriously unreliable science in Scotland. The Mountain Rescue Service provides a regularly updated report that is better than most. There are also avalanche watches in spring, which divert climbers and walkers away from black spots.

• Let someone know of your intended route and when you expect to be back.

• Take a map and compass and don't change your route along the way.

• Don't go on your own.

Do not think that taking a mobile phone is a substitute for wandering off poorly equipped. In the last couple of years, the mountain rescue has been inundated with calls from disorientated walkers stuck on mountains with little more than a pair of flip flops and a T-shirt. Go prepared and don't cry wolf just because you have a cell phone and know that you can.

Of course meticulous precautions and planning can go too far. I remember a couple of professional-looking hillwalkers mapping out their day's route. Dressed impeccably for the hill they were taking no chances. They had bright Gore-Tex clothes, head torches, gleaming boots, ice axes, and ski poles to aid balance. They stood pouring over a detailed laminated map setting compass bearings for the top of the nearby mountain. What confounded the scene was the absence of snow and the big signpost that they stood next to clearly pointing out the path that led straight to the peak.

STALKING AND SHOOTING

If climbing, walking, or driving through nature isn't entertaining enough, you can always opt to stalk it. "Stalking, shooting 'n fishing" is an ancient pastime in Scotland that still holds immense appeal.

Wild animals have provided an essential source of protein to the Scots from the earliest times when the Pictish people hunted deer by driving herds of them off cliffs. Discarded deer bones have been found in settlement remains dating back 7,000 years.

With the advent of supermarkets, shooting and stalking wild game has long since become a recreational sport. And yet it is more than a sport. It is a kind of ritual, tied up with tradition, social custom, and controversy. Getting involved takes much more than a steady aim, you have to also be sensitive to the currents that underlie the sport itself.

The term *stalking* in Scotland refers to hunting deer with high-powered rifles. Shooting describes shooting grouse with shotguns. Fox hunting with dogs on horseback is also a popular pastime in Britain. Fox hunting in Scotland, however, does not extend far beyond the borders with England where it is most commonly practised.

Stalking and shooting is carried out on the big estates. These estates own huge tracts of Scotland, which they maintain for sheep farming and blood sports. This means that civilisation doesn't encroach on the deer's natural habitat of high moor. Moorland grouse also feed themselves on heather and every season the old heath is burnt off to ensure fresh growth.

The red grouse lives in relative peace for most of the year in groups (or coveys) in deep heather. This all changes on August 12 (known as the glorious twelfth), when the hunting season for grouse is declared open across the country. Groups set out to walk over set areas (known as beats), shooting grouse that fly into their line of fire. Alternatively, some groups stand in wait in a small trench (known as a *butt*) to shoot grouse as they fly over. The grouse are driven over by beaters further down the valley. Gun dogs, mainly labradors are used to flush out the birds, and then pick them out of the long heather after they have been brought down.

The members of the shooting party, or guns, break for a pack lunch in the middle of the day and then swing back for home, shooting as they go. At the end of the day they compare their individual tallies, counted in pairs or braces, and comment on how the day went. A hundred years ago thousands of grouse would be shot in a single day by a few guns. These days disease, climatic change, and arguably overshooting, has taken its toll. Grouse populations are in gradual decline.

The king of all Scottish game beasts is in no such trouble. Red deer, native to Scotland, are so plentiful that they have to be culled each year to keep numbers down to a manageable level. Much of the Highlands are infertile high moor, and this is the habitat that is ideal for the herds of deer, that thrive in Scotland's bleak heights. They have done so well that overcrowding has left them 25% lighter

An old shooting lodge in Perthshire.

in weight now than they were 100 years ago. They are also much more prone to illness. Each year the big estates are obliged to shoot hundreds of deer, usually picking off the old and infirm to keep numbers under control. Most of the stalking is done in the month of October.

Much of this task falls to the estate gamekeeper, particularly when it comes to shooting the hinds in the winter months. However many sportsmen and women look forward to shooting stags during their mating season (or *rut*) in October. It is a skilful task, one that requires a lot of stamina.

The thrill comes from silently stalking a stag on your hands and knees, dressed from head to toe in camouflage to avoid being spotted. The gamekeeper, or stalker, is invariably on hand to help the shooter get to a hundred or so metres from the unsuspecting beast and to give the go ahead if he thinks it's a clear shot. There is no greater shame than wounding a beast and letting it get away.

Once shot, the deer is gutted, or "gralloched," on the hill and then transported to the butcher. If the stag is a handsome beast and has an impressive set of antlers he can look forward to having his head set on a plaque to be admired by future sportsmen and curious children. It's worth noting that when you shoot your first stag, or grouse for that matter, you can expect to have your face marked with the blood of your first kill. It's called being *blooded*.

After a stalking or shooting holiday, it is customary to tip the gamekeeper, after all it was probably his or her skill that led you to your prey in the first place. Often struggling to make a living from hill farming during the rest of the year, tips are an important supplement to a gamekeeper's income. Expect to give between £10 and £50 a day for grouse shooting and about £50 for a day of stalking. It's best to give a tip discreetly, in the form of a handshake and an envelope.

The Sporting Estate

Blood sports in Scotland are traditionally reserved for the upper classes. Stalking and shooting became a popular pastime for the well-heeled in 19th century Victorian Scotland, after Queen Victoria fell in love with the Highlands and first leased the Balmoral estate in 1844. The estate remains a much-loved retreat for present-day royalty.

With the royal seal of approval, the pursuit of aristocratic blood sports became a litmus paper for high social standing. After centuries of indifference to the Highlands, rich industrialists from the South, British blue blood—and their money—flowed North.

Suddenly, deer stalking and grouse shooting was big business, bringing much needed income to the big estates at a time when rural Scotland was suffering from agricultural depression. The amount of estate land set aside almost exclusively for stalking and shooting increased dramatically. Between 1883 and 1912 the average estate size doubled and the Highlands were increasingly allowed to return to open moor as it is today, ideal for grouse and deer.

Many sporting lodges have changed hands in recent years. They have become increasingly expensive to run privately. Multinational companies have bought many sporting lodges to run as businesses for corporate entertainment. The big organisations concerned with conservation, such as The National Trust and the John Muir Trust, are also big landowners now. Only a few of the old estates remain in private hands.

There is something oddly British about all that bruising physical discomfort and fortitude against capricious weather and rough ground. The old whisky-soaked, tweed-draped duffer complete with pipe, red nose, and his faithful dog has become an enduring caricature of the Scottish Highlands.

Bloodsports are no less exclusive these days than in the 19th century. Expect to spend an average of £250 for each stag shot and up to £110 for a driven brace of grouse, and this is before counting accommodation and food.

There is a reassuring sense of tradition to a full day's shooting. On returning to a lodge after a day's shooting, hot baths are lined up, and everyone changes to more formal dress for the evening ahead. Tea and cake is served, followed a little later by drinks and then a formal three-course meal with all the trimmings. Dinner is usually a cheery and noisy affair of stories, jokes, speeches, and toasts. And of course the port is passed around at the end of every meal.

The clothing required for stalking and shooting has changed little over the centuries. Standard uniform on the hill includes a checked shirt, a waxed jacket, and often a cloth cap to complete the look. Men and women don plus-fours, which are tweed trousers that stop just below the knee. Long socks are pulled up over the calf to provide protection from the elements. Twenty-first century outdoor wear such as bright Gore-Tex jackets, is lost on this crowd who see it as being somehow impractical.

James, a Scottish friend who works in an outdoor centre told me that after the advent of light and durable artificial fibres some years ago, he never imagined that people still wore all that heavy tweed on the hill. That was until he visited a lodge and came face to face with a shooting party who seemed to him as though they had stepped straight out of another century.

You will have probably noticed that women have had little mention in this section. Bloodsports are predominantly male dominated. This isn't to say that women are excluded; they aren't and if they do take part they are often the keenest shots. It's just that the sport has more appeal to the hunting instincts of men. Girlfriends, daughters, and wives play the no less important role of making sure that their men don't take themselves, and their guns, too seriously.

Land and People

Stalking and shooting draw strong critics in Scotland and around the world. Talk to a cross section of society and you will hear passionate arguments for and against, but seldom indifference. It's not surprising considering the sport is so intimately tied up with class, land, and ultimately politics.

The most emotive debate surrounds the issue of land. A few wealthy individuals have owned much of Scotland ever since the Norman conquerors first carved up the country for themselves in the 13th century. My own well-known Scottish name, Grant, comes from a family of French nobles called Le Grand who were given the area around Inverness to lord over. Eventually they intermarried with the locals and went native. Patterns of land ownership have changed little since, with a few estates owning much of rural Scotland. Many feel resentful that the old estates cleared their tenants to make way for the more profitable sheep farming and blood sports.

Today's figures on land ownership speak for themselves. There are around 14 million acres of land in Scotland for a population of 5 million people. Of all this land, 1,252 landowners, 0.25% of the population, own over two thirds of all the rural land.

Plenty of Scots would be happy to see an end to sporting estates, considered by many to be big playgrounds for the rich. Advocates of sporting estates are just as vocal. The pro-blood sports lobby points out that stalking and shooting brings essential cash and jobs to isolated areas of Scotland. Much of the land that makes it possible for deer to thrive is too poor to do anything else with apart from converting it into forestry plantations. The argument goes that it is the way the large estates manage their land that has conserved the natural beauty and wildlife that we have come to take for granted in Scotland.

And so the debates have gone round in circles for generations, although the tradition of sporting estates is somewhat on the back foot at the moment. With national parks now set up by the Scottish Executive in Loch Lomond and the Cairngorms the pattern of land ownership may be set change. Fox hunting with dogs may also be banned although stalking and grouse shooting are not threatened. It looks like twenty-first century issues are finally catching up with this most Victorian of pastimes.

FISHING

An Ode to the Mighty Salmon:

> lonesome traveller
> roaming your underworld
> of rock and dark waters
> jumping clear
> of falling torrents
> unhindered, unerred
> in the pitch
> of an ancient night
>
> rested and yet restless
> in your eddy
> your backwater
> of silvering light
> a muddy shallow
> from the ocean
> that cradled you
> destined to survive
> a bony act of will
> destined to die
> exhausted on a
> grassy bank
> tricked by a feather
> betrayed at dusk
> floundered, sunk
> on a quivering line.

lonesome traveller
your spirit merges
mountains with sea
the sky with this broken stream
and death with life
with life
itself

—Author

Salmon inspire awe and respect in equal measure from fishermen and women who cast their long lines into Scotland's rivers in the hope of landing one. Success is never assured as they are notoriously difficult to catch.

Salmon "run" up Scotland's rivers from spring until late autumn. They spend the rest of the year fattening up in the Atlantic somewhere off the Greenland shelf. They travel up Highland rivers, covering up to 25 km (15.5 miles) a day, to spawn and return, or to die. The bigger, slow flowing peaty rivers in the east such as the Dee, Tay, and the Spey offer the best fishing.

Salmon of all shapes and sizes swim up these rivers and are named according to their age or condition. The baby parr are no more than a few months old, the smolts are up to two-years-old, and a mature salmon lives until it is about six-years-old. A spent salmon, meaning a fish that has spawned and is heading back to sea, is called a *kelt*. To confuse matters even further, a male salmon is called a *cock* and a female salmon a *hen*.

Despite the best efforts of fishermen and scientists, the Atlantic salmon remains a mystery. No one knows for certain why they search out exactly where they were born to return to and spawn again. Nor why they come into the rivers' lower reaches on a full moon's high tide. Experienced fishermen will even tell you that they even predict the weather, rushing through a shallow stretch of river just before a dry spell makes it impassable.

Willie MacGregor, an experienced gamekeeper on a Highland estate best summed up what's known about these elusive creatures in his own inimitable style. He said, "If I wrote a book entitled *How Much I Know About Salmon Fishing*, by Willie MacGregor, the contents would be a single blank page." This is hardly surprising given that no one can even explain why salmon take the fisherman's fly in the first place as they don't eat a thing while coursing upstream to their spawning grounds.

Environmental pressures increasingly threaten wild salmon. The number of salmon in Scottish rivers has been in steady decline since about a century ago when they were so plentiful that farmers used to feed them to the pigs. In the last year, the situation has taken a dramatic turn for the worse with a sharp drop in wild salmon catches reported in rivers in the west coast of the Highlands. According to WWF-Scotland, some 300 of Scotland's 2,000 rivers are now empty of salmon.

Netting salmon in big numbers in sea estuaries has virtually stopped, and these days many fishermen return their catches to the river, especially the hens. But the reasons for the salmon's decline are more complicated than just overfishing. Much of the blame has been placed on salmon farms polluting inshore waters with chemicals and spreading disease from farmed salmon to their wild cousins. Whatever the reason, the possibility of Scotland's rivers becoming empty of salmon, like many in England and North America, is no longer a remote one.

Tight Lines—Fly Fishing for Salmon in Scotland

Fishing for salmon in Scotland with a small imitation fly on a long fly rod has been popular since the 19th century. Salmon are much easier to catch with live bait or a lure. In fact, poachers, use everything from nets to poison to catch salmon in the dead of night. But it is fly fishing that is considered the proper way to fish for salmon, and it requires great patience and skill.

The art of fly-fishing lies in pitting yourself against a prey that has even odds of getting away. It is a real contest, a battle of wills. There is a whole science to fly fishing, with enough books written on techniques to clog up the very estuaries themselves. For more information on the finer points of different flies, casting, and optimum light and weather conditions please refer to the bibliography at the back of this book.

One thing is for certain, being a good salmon fisherman, or woman, requires much more than skill and good luck. You need a reflective temperament to pass an often uneventful day by a quietly flowing river. One anonymous author writing on his passion best summed up the sports' job description. He said, "The chief qualities required are patience, a love of nature to enable you to appreciate the surroundings and the bird life, keenness, and of course, plenty of time and complete disregard of the weather. Without this you'll never be a fisherman."

It's funny the quote should end with the word "fisherman" when many claim that women have the best luck. The record for the biggest salmon caught using a fly in British waters is held by a Mrs Morrison on the River Deveron in October 1924. The beast weighed an awesome 28 kg (61 pounds)! There is even a theory that female pheromones lure the salmon onto their lines, causing much chagrin amongst the fraternity of male fishermen.

Finding a spot to fish for salmon legally can be tricky as fishing rights in Scotland bear no relation to land ownership. Many sporting estates offer fishing as part of the shooting-stalking package mentioned above, but this is not guaranteed.

Most of the fishing is divided into beats, or stretches of riverbank, which are hired out in week-long blocks during the season. Established fishermen are offered the same beat year in and year out making it hard for newcomers to find a space. Applying for a beat is a slow and complicated process that involves getting onto a tenancy list of a river's letting agent or proprietor.

The best bet is to get invited onto someone else's beat or to go directly to the river's gamekeeper, or ghillie, for a day's licence. Every salmon river has one or more ghillies. Their job is to husband the waters, watching out for poachers and limiting the number of fishermen on each stretch of water. They also have an intuitive knowledge of their rivers' elusive travellers, offering advice on the best spots to fish and on the finer arts of actually landing one.

Salmon fishing isn't cheap. Catching a salmon on one of the big name rivers costs as much as £10,000 pounds! Fish one of the smaller rivers with less salmon and you can expect to pay between £12 and £80 for a day's licence.

Trout and Pike Fishing

Fishing for the salmon's poorer cousin, the humble brown trout, holds less appeal but can be just as satisfying. Where the salmon rivers are well managed and easily accessible, catching trout often just involves a long tramp up to an isolated river or loch. Trout may be smaller and easier to catch than salmon, especially if you use a spinning rod with a bright lure instead of a fly, but they are just as tasty.

In recent years fisheries for the North American rainbow trout have sprung up, mainly on the borders and in central Scotland. For a fee you can throw a fly in one of these small, well-stocked lakes with a greater chance of catching something than if you are fishing for the wilder and wilier brown trout.

Pike, denizens of the deep, are the ugliest fresh water fish in Scotland. The Endrick Pike Head on display at the Kelvingrove Art Gallery in Glasgow looks like a primitive version of the monster from the film *Aliens*. The head is all that's left of the 113 kg (70 pound) beast found in 1934. Pike are caught with a big lure, dead bait, or even a bit of cheese. They make for a smelly, bone infested meal, but are tasty if eaten very fresh.

The closed season for trout in Scotland is from October 7 to March 14, both days inclusive. Many areas extend these dates to give trout stocks more time to recover. Licences to fish trout or pike are much easier to get hold of than those for salmon fishing and are much cheaper. Most country hotels and tackle shops sell licences for between £5 and £25 for a day. A rod licence is not required in Scotland. The Orkney Isles is the only place where you don't need a licence, and can just cast a line into the waters.

GOLF IS GREAT

Walking across Edinburgh's central parkland, the Meadows, one winter evening, I saw a man holding a golf club in the half-light of a drizzly night gazing intensely at a point in the distance. He steadied himself and swung. The golf ball flew off and neatly landed a hundred yards on, between lampposts and the folk walking home from work. The man cursed, set down another ball and thwacked it off again in the same uncertain direction, barely discernible in the failing light. There was something about the disregard the man had for the rain, encroaching night, or the people walking home liable to bizarre injury that sums up just how seriously golf can be taken in Scotland. And what better place to play if you have the itch.

Golf has been with Scotland for a very long time. In fact, Scots often make the proud boast that they invented golf. This isn't strictly true. Golf, or *kolf* as it was then termed, was a popular pastime among the Scots and Dutch. In medieval times, they aimed at specific trees for competition instead of thwacking balls down holes. Scotland was the birthplace of golf with holes in the ground as a target, and the rest is history…

The earliest written references to golf in Scotland date back to 1457 when King James banned the game (along with soccer) because it was keeping his subjects away from archery practice. Few people paid much notice though, and by the 17th century, the sport of golf was in full swing.

Most passionate golfers make the pilgrimage to St Andrews, a small and picturesque town in Fife on the East Coast. The Old Course

Beware, too much golf can be hazardous to your health!

running alongside the sea just outside the town is hallowed ground for golfers. Play there and you walk in step with most of the masters of the past. In June 2000 it was Tiger Woods' turn, winning the British Open competition on the Old Course with a typically comfortable margin. Some 80,000 fans turned out to watch.

Although there are golf courses scattered around Scotland, St Andrews remains the undisputed home of golf. Where else can they boast of no less than six courses, designed for varying levels of fitness and skill. St Andrews is also the home of the National Golf Museum which holds a stunning array of glass cases filled with dissected golf balls. These displays offer detailed explanations of the advances in ball technology over the years.

There is much more to golfing in Scotland than just St Andrews. The variety of courses, usually set in breathtaking surroundings, makes the whole country a great draw for enthusiasts. There are the typical seaside links courses such as Troon, Dornoch, Nairn, Muirfield, and Gullane. Parkland courses such as Pitlochry and Machrihanish offer a mix of trees, ponds, and lakes. Then of course there are the Highland courses such as Gleneagles and Loch Lomond to add to the list.

Part of the appeal of golfing in Scotland is also the challenge. Wild weather and less manicured fairways makes the game more demanding but also more rewarding than in many other countries.

Golf in Scotland caters for every pocket. Expect to pay as little as £1.50 a round on one of the smaller courses in the low season and as much as £100 for a round on the most prestigious courses, such as the Old Course or Gleneagles.

The green fees for a round of nine or 18 holes is paid to a club's resident professional golfer in the pro-shop. You can buy equipment and hire clubs, buggies, manual trolleys, or even electrical caddy carts there.

Caddies have to be booked in advance and are paid between £20 and £50 a round depending on their experience. If you play well and feel the caddy has been suitably encouraging, expect to give a tip of between 10% and 25% of his or her fee. Always give a note rather than loose coins.

Playing golf in Scotland if you are a complete newcomer to the game is not easy. Most clubhouses will not allow play unless the golfer has a handicap certificate. This is the average number of strokes it takes an individual to get around a course, over and above the course's par. To get a handicap you have to join a golf club and have your ability assessed over a few rounds before being given a certificate. Even then, the most prestigious courses are often not for beginners. Men need to have a handicap under 24 and ladies under 36 to play the Old Course.

Becoming a member of a golf club in Scotland takes persistence. The first port of call is the club's secretary, who interviews prospective members. If you are deemed suitable, you will then be invited to apply, so it is important to humbly explain your motives for joining rather than bluntly declare that you wish to be a member. The next step is to find two existing members who are willing to propose and second your application. The more prestigious courses require up to ten members seconding an application.

Next, you will be asked to play a round of golf with at least two members. You have to demonstrate to them that you know the rules of the game and aren't completely hopeless on the course, holding everyone else up behind you. It is also important to show the right sporting spirit, not swearing blindly and tearing chunks out of the green if you miss a hit but saying things like 'good shot' when your opponent is making mincemeat of you.

Even if you jump all these hurdles you may still have to wait. Many clubs have waiting lists that are up to 20 years long. In fact some club members put their children down on the list when they are born, so that if they develop a passion for the game they can become club members themselves by the time they are twenty.

Those who are invited to join are expected to pay twice the annual subscription as an entrance fee. Annual membership varies between £100 and £1,500 depending on the course but after that you can play as much as you like for no additional fee. Friends and family can play at discounted rates. You have to own your own golf clubs and shoes.

Traditions in golf are almost as important as the game itself in Scotland. So much so that each course has its own peculiarities. It's worth phoning a clubhouse in advance to find out if there are any surprises. For example, there are a few clubs that still admit men only, and the most prestigious can insist that visitors play with a member. To play a round on the Old Course, your name has to be picked out of a ballot on the morning that you are due to tee off.

Lunch is common to all of the clubhouses. In the 18th century, a three- to four-hour feast typically followed a round in the morning. Golf, business, and eating were so interlinked in those days, that members were fined if they didn't turn up to dine after playing.

These days the social side to golf isn't so strictly enforced but remains just as important. A round of golf, lasting an average of three hours, is usually played before or after lunch in the clubhouse. It is a good idea to choose and order lunch, even if it is only a sandwich, well in advance to avoid a long wait.

Dress sense is not as formal as in Victorian times when women wore long frocks and hats and men sported shirt and tie, a smart Norfolk jacket and cap. On the course, men and women are expected to wear a shirt with a collar and a pair of slacks. Jeans are not allowed. Most courses require spiked golf shoes that don't tear up the greens. The clubhouse's mixed bar and restaurant requires a jacket, shirt, and tie for the men and equally smart attire for the women, usually a dress.

To this day, golf remains something of a man's world. Women used to be barred from most courses and a curt sign still reads "No ladies or dogs" on the entrance to the Royal and Ancient clubhouse in St Andrews. Most clubhouses still have a men-only spike bar for drinks straight off the course. The ladies have to get changed first, before meeting up in the mixed bar later.

Although there are many keen lady golfers, the sport's traditional image of men with moustaches is hard to shake off. Nor is the attitude many older golfers have to the ladies. On being told that the men-only bar was to be done away with in his club house, one old timer said, "It's not the ladies that I object to, it's the bloody women."

Then there are those who object to the game itself. Ever since King James banned golf in favour of archery practice, golfers have been gently chided for "ruining a good walk." When I asked golf enthusiast Roger Wood, sadly no relation to Tiger Woods, what he had to say to those who thought that the whole business was an expensive waste of time, he leapt eloquently to the game's defence. "It's much more fun to practice mind over matter than to walk in a vacuum," he said.

A Brief Glossary of Golfing Terms

Albatross—Extremely rare just like the bird, this denotes a score of three shots under par.

Birdie—One under par.

Bogey—One stroke over par. A bogey is a frightening mythical figure that Golfers imagined themselves playing against when fixed scores for each hole were first introduced.

Bunker—Sand dune.

Caddie—The wee man or woman who carries the clubs and offers advice on the round.

Fore!—Shouted out to warn other players of imminent danger from a mishit ball.

Green fees—The amount you pay for a round of golf.

Handicap—You can't play on a proper golf course without a handicap. This is the number over the course par (average) that it usually takes you to get round the course. This means that the worse you play, the higher your handicap and the more strokes you have to get round. Therefore if you play a better golfer your skill levels are balanced, as he or she will have a lower handicap and therefore less strokes in which to get round the course in.

Hole in one—Long distance fluke shot when the ball is holed with a single stroke.

In the rough—When the ball is in the rough ground off the fairway.

Irons—Golf clubs used to take medium-range shots. In the 19th century each one had a name of its own and you would have had to choose between a mid mashie, mashie niblick or cleek.

Links—A coastal course. Many famous golf courses in Scotland are links courses.

The rub of the green—A common expression used to describe fickle weather conditions or bounces that make golf such an unpredictable and challenging sport.

Spike bar—Bar in the clubhouse that you don't need to change from the course to enter.

Spikes—Golfers shoes with spikes on them.

Par—Meaning the "usual or average" this is the standard set score in strokes for each hole.

Parkland/ Highland courses—Inland settings for Golf courses.

Putter—The stick for the final moment(s) on the putting green.

Scratch golfer—A golfer with a handicap of zero.

Wood—Golf clubs with wooden bases used for long-range shots.

SHINTY

Golf isn't Scotland's only homegrown sport. The sport of shinty, known as *camanachd* in Gaelic, is as old as Christianity's first awakenings in the Highlands. Introduced by Irish missionaries over two thousand years ago, the game has thrived ever since.

Shinty is a fast passing game with stick and ball between two teams over 90 minutes. Aiming for their opponents' goals, players hit a cork-filled leather ball in the air or on the ground. The game is fast and physical, looking like a cross between hockey, golf, and Australian Rules football. There is one theory that the curved sticks, called *camans*, used by players inspired the invention of golf itself.

Shinty is most popular in and around the town of Newtonmore in the central Highlands. It's here that the Camanachd Association was founded in 1877 and where the yearly tussles with local rival Kingussie is played out for the Camanachd Cup.

THE HIGHLAND GAMES

Type "The Highland Games" into an Internet search engine and references to it will pop up all over the world. It seems the game has travelled with homesick Highlanders to all the corners of the Earth. That's not surprising for a sport that is so quintessentially Scottish—a gritty trial of Herculean strengths with ball, hammer, and caber (a tree trunk). Not to mention a piping competition that, according to one friend, "…puts to shame even the fiercest of catfights."

The oldest games didn't actually originate in the Highlands. Ceres in Fife first put on a show of strength in 1314 to celebrate the return of their 600 bowmen, triumphant from the battle of Bannockburn. The games nowadays are a mix of brawn, skill, and dexterity. The main Herculean tests are throwing the hammer, tossing the caber, and tug of wars. The lighter events are sprinting, fell running (running up hills), pole-vaulting, and jumping. There is also room for invention—some days include anything from sheepdog trials and shinty to clay pigeon shooting or even pillow fighting.

The opening ceremony of a Highland games is a colourful pageant of dancing and piping. Highland dress is worn by many competitors—except of course, those competing in the pole vault. About 60 games are held across Scotland every year from July through September.

Tossing the Cow Pat

Humour also plays its part in Scottish outdoor sports. A lesser known but no less bitterly contested competition is the national cow pat (manure) throwing competition. A suitably dry specimen is chosen for its weight and aerodynamics, and is thrown like a discus by young Adonises. The furthest throw wins the coveted trophy.

A friend still has his in a dusty cupboard from when he was crowned champion back in 1984. "The last man to throw got 108 feet," he recounted. "I stepped up and threw 113 feet, in fact I threw the cow pat so well it flew on past the perimeter and bounced off a car bonnet." Interviewed afterwards on national television my friend put his big moment down to "a lucky throw."

SNOW LINES

From late October, snow starts dusting the mountaintops in the Highlands. By November the downhill skiing season is in full swing, although the best snowfalls tend to come in January and February.

There are five ski centres in Scotland. These are the Nevis Range and Glencoe to the west and Glenshee, the Lecht, and Cairngorm over to the east. In the winter, the village of Aviemore becomes something of a glamorous resort, with skiers enjoying Swiss chalet-style accommodation and easy access to the Cairngorm, the Lecht, and Glenshee.

Skiing in these centres may not be as good, or as exotic, as the big resorts in continental Europe but it is more affordable. An average day pass is around £20 for adults and £10 for children. The centres also offer all-inclusive packages with five days board, skiing, hire, and tuition costing as little as £150.00 per adult.

It's worthwhile checking the snow conditions on a daily basis before committing yourself to a day's skiing in Scotland. Conditions are unpredictable and you can find yourself enjoying pristine powder snow one day followed by a combination of rock, heather, slush and sheet ice the next. Scottish skiers tend to drive up to one of the centres for the day after a heavy snowfall.

Chapter Nine

THE HIGHLAND AND ISLANDS

"In the north, on a showery day, you can see the rain, its lovely behaviour over an island—while you stand a mile off in a patch of sun."
—George Mackay Brown, *An Orkney Tapestry*

How times have changed. In the space of a couple of hundred years the image of the Highlands has changed from being a feared frontier land inhabited by roving savages to a place of romance and beauty. Thanks to Sir Walter Scott's swashbuckling novels of the 19th century, such as *Waverley* and *Rob Roy*, the far north stands in popular imagination as a romantic notion of paradise lost. In "Scott" land the lassies are always "bonnie," and the glens eternally dappled with sunlight and topped with proud stags, known on postcards as Monarchs of the Glen.

Travel to the Highlands and it's hard to see past the clichés. The tourist board feeds the average visitor with quaint images of tartan and shortbread. Visitors' centres tell of heroic battles and the daring escape by the ever-dashing Bonnie Prince Charlie. Driving through the fantastic scenery seems to confirm it all.

Getting any closer to an actual past or present in the Highlands is trickier. You have to look with an unblinking eye, unclouded by the rich mosaic of misconceptions that makes the region such a popular destination.

That there is a Highlands and a Lowlands in Scotland is the first undisputed place to start. Geography makes the reality unassailable. A single fault line that runs diagonally from Stonehaven in the East to Dunoon in the West neatly divides Scotland. To the south the Lowlands offer a softer, greener landscape, while to the north, the rolling hills give way to a wilderness of mountains, lochs, bogs, and heaths.

THE HIGHLANDER

Beyond the rugged contours of the Highlands, the sharpest contrast that distinguishes the area from southern Scotland is people, or rather the absence of them. Most of the population is squeezed into the central belt of Edinburgh, Glasgow, and the scattering of towns in between. Further north there are whole valleys or glens bereft of inhabitants. Most Scots still have the old clan names, such as MacGregor or MacDuff, but the Highlanders of *Braveheart* fame have long since moved on.

What happened to the ancient population of the Highlands, where they were dispersed to and why, is a very long story that has been told countless times and with countless distortions. But despite the miles of print already reeled off on Highland history, the tale still needs a brief retelling. Events such as the Jacobite uprisings and the clearances cannot be ignored because they have left too deep an impression on the Highlands and how they are perceived.

The clans were tribes of people, bonded by blood and land, who lived and fought together under a single family name. Fiercely independent, each clan answered solely to their chief (or laird), and spent more time quarrelling with their neighbours than taking on the English. They were entirely self-sufficient, living off their own crops, game, and Highland cattle, often raided from their neighbours.

This clan system of local autonomy only survived into the 18th century as the Highlands were too inaccessible for laws, kings, and tax collectors to make any lasting impression. However sooner or later, the growth of the nation state, coupled with boundless imperial progress was going to come up against this ragtag army of feudal tribesmen who didn't want to pay homage to any leader but their own. That moment came with decisive brutality in the summer of 1746.

The Jacobite rebellions of the 17th and 18th centuries hold a powerful place in Scottish memory. Remembered in song, taught at school in the Highlands, and marked with little crossed swords for the battles won and lost on tourist maps, the romance of Bonnie Prince Charlie's rebellion and the fallen clansmen at the Battle of Culloden still lives on.

That the Highlanders' struggle ended in tragedy gives the whole episode a particularly charged feel. The actual events are a little more confusing. Why the landing of a young Frenchman with seven companions in a small boat in Knoydart in June 1745 led to the virtual annihilation of an entire way of life needs a little explanation.

Prince Charles Edward Stuart (also called Bonnie Prince Charlie, or the Young Pretender), was only the latest in a long line of Scottish Stuart princes who tried to reclaim the English throne by raising invading armies in the Highlands.

The Stuarts were Scotland's, and arguably England's rightful kings. James Stuart I of England, who was also James Stuart VI of Scotland, succeeded Elizabeth I, and governed the whole island with little opposition from 1603. However James' son Charles I and grandson Charles II were both arrogant and ineffectual rulers. For a start, they were Catholics in a predominantly Protestant country. To make matters worse, they espoused the divine right of kings to absolute power, putting them at odds with the nobles in Parliament who wanted more say in government. Charles I ended up being beheaded at the hands of Cromwell in 1640, and his son James II was deposed by the Dutch protestant William of Orange in 1688.

These Stuart kings may not have had the Highlander's best interests at heart, but from exile in France they were quick to exploit support in the far north for their cause, which was known as the Jacobite cause. Resentment toward the union of the crowns, and with it the loss of Scottish sovereignty in 1709, had promoted a string of failed Jacobite rebellions before Charles made his reckless bid for the crown in 1745.

Charles' support was always much patchier than is commonly imagined. If the whole of the Highlands had marched to his banner, the historian John Prebble estimates that he could have raised 63,000 men, easily enough to march all the way into London. Internal rivalry and division meant that there were never more than 5,000 to 6,000 on the march at one time.

They still came close to toppling King George I from the English throne, who was a German from the Hanovarian line. Prince Charles' army made it as far south as Derby in Northern England in December 1745. King George was so worried that he was prepared to flee the country had the Highland army marched on London. Instead they retreated, giving George time to regroup and, at the hands of his son the Duke of Cumberland, inflicting a final solution on the restless natives of the north.

The defining moment for the fate of the Highlands came on a boggy area of ground called Drummossie Moor at Culloden outside Inverness. It was there the English forces, better fed and equipped, and greater in number, met a demoralised and exhausted Highland army on April 16, 1746.

The site of the battle at Culloden, which is now a popular visitors' centre, has an eerie feel to it. The mass graves of the fallen clansmen are marked with small headstones, and legend has it that heather never grows on these grassy mounds. The battleground flutters with flags marking the positions of the two armies before the Highlanders' desperate charge. It is hard to imagine that the course of so much history could have been channelled into such a narrow patch of desolate moor.

The Highlanders' charge that day, their only battle tactic, fell short on the flat ground against a barrage of musket and cannon fire. Bonnie Prince Charlie, whose poor military planning had caused the massacre, fled a field spilt with the blood and hopes of a generation of clansmen. As well as the estimated 1,000 killed on Culloden moor, some 1,150 were shipped abroad and countless others executed in the weeks that followed the battle.

The Highlanders were loyal to their prince to the very last. Till today, Bonnie Prince Charlie is remembered in story and song as the noble hero, fleeing capture by the English forces across the Highlands. He managed to escape back to France from the Isle of Skye disguised in the clothes of the young Scottish woman, Flora MacDonald.

The real story is in what happened after Charlie left. In a series of punitive laws passed by Parliament in the years following the rebellion, known as the Concessions of the Act of Union, the Highland way of life and culture was brutally suppressed. Wearing tartan, speaking Gaelic, or even playing the bagpipes were banned. Land owned by anyone who had supported the Jacobite cause was confiscated. Army barracks, some still standing as bleak ruins to this day, were erected outside communities to house government troops in case of further trouble. The old clan ways were effectively outlawed.

With the collapse of the clan structure in the aftermath of Culloden, clan chiefs or lairds increasingly played the role of traditional landlords, exploiting the people on their lands rather than protecting them.

They chose to fill their glens with the far more profitable Cheviot and black-faced sheep rather than people. Termed "the Clearances," thousands of poor tenant farmers were forcibly evicted and herded into boats bound for the colonies from the 1840s to the 1860s. The sheep that replaced them were nicknamed *four-footed clansmen*, since there were so few actual clansmen and women left.

Blaming the emptying out of the Highlands in the 19th century on greedy landlords alone is short of the whole picture however. Many chose to leave, unable to manage even subsistence farming because of the poor soil, especially when there were plenty of jobs in the new industries in the cities.

But that thousands were rounded up and exported is beyond dispute. Many deserted glens with the remains of old stone home-steads are a legacy of the Clearances. I remember exploring the old crofts behind our cottage, abandoned since the owners were evicted over 150 years ago. The remains of an old pot and some utensils were still buried in the hearth of the fire. Whoever was there can't have had time to take anything with them; they were simply dragged out and marched onto the waiting boats for the New World. Sometimes their homes were burnt behind them.

Paradise Lost

It's easy to forget how the Highlanders were once viewed as a fierce and unruly threat to the established order of things. To most people in the south they were thought of as a barbarous people to be civilised, not unlike the diverse other peoples throughout the world that came under British colonial rule in the 19th century.

It was only after they had been vanquished that they took on the role of tragic victims in the popular imagination. These very same people who had once been called "barbarian clans" became the romantic heroes of a paradise lost. The Highlands were transformed into a charming and romantic landscape and the popular tourist destination that it remains today.

Regret over the loss of the old Highland way of life can be compared to modern attitudes about the lost cultures of the Native Americans. Both peoples have since been immortalised as a symbol of a way of living the modern industrial world has lost. The clans of the Highlands will always be romanticised, seen through the coloured lenses of regret for a vanished world, like the fading paintings of tartan-clad men fighting to their last breath on Culloden Moor.

THE HIGHLANDS TODAY

Living in the Highlands today is far removed from visiting a Scottish city. So distinct is the experience that short stories, factual accounts, novels, and reams of poems have been written about the people, times, and traditions in the far north. For the unsuspecting visitor the shock of the first encounter is a peculiar and complex one, an odd mix of heart-stopping beauty, romance, magic, and frustration.

The first thing that impresses itself on you in the Highlands is the silence. Coming from a busy urban centre like London or New York, the contrast is breathtaking. Lying in the deep heather on a mountainside or on a beach on the west coast, you could be forgiven for thinking you are one of the world's first human settlers. That is, until the moment is shattered by the Highlands' biggest birds of prey—Royal Air Force jets that skim in under low cloud like silent arrows. I remember once when on the road that goes past the Clunie Dam we saw a jet flying over the water below the level of our car.

Jets or no jets, the Highlands have a serenity that modern cities lack, and this silence and space draws many to live up north. June Crocker grew up and spent her working life in Orpington, outside of London. When she retired as a schoolteacher, she and her husband remembered an enchanting holiday in Argyllshire and left everything to move there.

Now settled in the village of Ardfern, June has no regrets. She told me, "It's the landscape that I fell in love with, it's never the same from one day to the next." There is something uniquely Scottish about the light and the colours of the west coast; no wonder so much romance, so many tales of love, heroism, and loss have come out of this land.

The spirit of independence and freedom still lives on in the land and people of the Highlands today. All those big open spaces bring with them the feel of a frontier land, a sort of modern-day wild west, only without gunslingers like Clint Eastwood and with a lot less sunshine than Wyoming.

Life here is unconstrained by many of the rules and regulations that order most people's lives in the rest of 21st century Britain. Highland people tend to speed in their cars without wearing seatbelts, often drink too much and too late, and have few dealings with the police. In short they have the space to live gloriously messy and unconventional lives.

It is like a breath of fresh air compared to the small-minded and constrained world further south. One Greek friend Maria, was amazed to find that when she first arrived in England she could hear the sound of traffic wherever she went. You are never far from a road in the south; open a road atlas of the southeast and your mind boggles at the complex crisscross of roads, roundabouts, and junctions. The few green spaces left feel like traffic islands.

One story goes a long way to illustrating the contrast between the Highlands and small-town life farther to the south. The story, published in a national paper, tells of a woman who was out walking her dog in a park in the town of Newton Abbot, in the southwest of England. As she was getting back in the car, her dog ran back with a small stick. Absentmindedly she threw the stick in the back of the car and drove home. Unfortunately the park warden spotted her "stealing" the stick. The warden reported the incident to the police who tracked the woman down. She was made to return the stick to the park in the presence of a police officer and verbally reprimanded by the park warden! This is an extreme example but it certainly would never happen in the far north. All those mountains bring a greater sense of perspective.

Song Lines to the High Road

There are few landscapes left in Europe where the past is as visible as the present. The Highlands is one of them. With limited interference from the urban industrial development of the modern world, previous lives linger on. History can be peeled back and exposed like the layers of an onion.

For example, if you stand in the Neolithic settlement remains of Skara Brae on Orkney, it's almost as though it was never deserted some 5,000 years ago by some of this island's first inhabitants. The beehive-like network of dwellings are still intact, complete with their stone trestle tables, cupboards for cooking utensils, and beds.

This visible contact with the past is perhaps the first and most lingering shock for foreign visitors. Aimi, a friend from New Zealand, was astounded when she came to spend a summer doing voluntary work on the Isle of Mull. Coming from a country with few historical traces of man, the oldest human remains she had seen were old whaling equipment from 200 years ago. "I just can't get my head round the sense of the past here, where some of the standing stones are over 5,000 years old," she once told me.

Nowhere is this more evident than on the tiny island of Iona. Viewed from the much bigger island of Mull, there seems nothing to it. It sits like a stone, cast away and long since disregarded. But this brief and boggy outcrop of land is charged with centuries of religious and political history.

Saint Columba first landed here from Ireland in A.D. 583, bringing with him Christianity and the missionary zeal to spread it east to the pagans across the rest of Scotland. The old Celtic crosses that blend Celtic and Christian symbols are still standing. But Iona is more than the meeting point of the Christian and pagan worlds. It is marked by the intersection of countless peoples and beliefs.

In the little museum by the graveyard, old Celtic crosses sit next to gravestones with carvings of medieval feudal knights resting their heads on stone pillows. Viking tombs depict their high-prowed ships and the eternal battle that will ensure their passage from the middle hearth to Valhalla. There are said to be six kings buried on the island, including Macbeth, all making their bids for immortality, at least in the memories of those that outlived them.

Visiting places like Iona in the Highlands is a sobering lesson in history, it brings home what a brief and fragile tenure we all have on this earth. Compared to all this history our lives seem a passing flicker with a finite end: earth and bones. The message isn't a depressing one, quite the opposite in fact—it can give you a healthy sense of perspective. "Being so conscious of our own mortality gives us all the more reason to celebrate life and make the most of the chance we have," Aimi once told me.

It also explains the proliferation stories of ghosts, ghouls, and witches that still haunt people's imaginations and perhaps the land itself. On Iona, every cove and mound has a name telling of some mythical or real encounter. Most chilling of all is the White Strand of the Monks, a long, white beach where 18 monks were ambushed and murdered by Viking raiders in the 9th century. Some locals claim their ghosts can still be seen walking the beach in a storm at dusk.

VILLAGE LIFE

If you are on the tourist trail in search of empty mountains, sombre lochs or standing stone remnants of the past, it is easy to forget that the Highlands are also a living breathing community. Life in a small village in the Highlands can offer a support network of friendly neighbours; a genuine sense of community in an age when so many live in huge anonymous cities.

"This is the best social life I've ever had, there is always something going on," Allison Gill, a resident of Tobermory on Mull told me. What newcomers to village life notice more than anything is how friendship crosses the generation gap. In a country dominated by youth culture, where the older generations are often forgotten by mainstream society, old people are genuinely cared for and respected.

"There is no age gap here, kids and old people get on, and you may even get old grannies dancing on the tables at parties," she said.

If you decide to settle in a Highland village you will need to accept that it may be impossible ever to be accepted as truly "local." Only people born into families who have been there for generations manage that. But the support system is still there for those who commit themselves to village life. A woman who lived in a small croft cottage up the hill from in us in Glenelg had married a local man and lived there for over 50 years, but she was still known as "That lass from Glasgow." However, when her time came to die, she had someone by her bed day and night, the local people all took turns to sit with her.

I remember the whole of our village turning out to celebrate an elderly resident's 100th birthday. I can still see old Mr Jardine at his front door in his wheelchair—he had lost a leg in World War I— met with cheers, fireworks and a big bonfire on the beach opposite.

Highland life also offers days free of the stresses and strains of the rat race, with time always short and everyone in a rush. The relativity of time becomes a glaring reality if you visit the Highlands from a fast moving metropolis like Tokyo, New York, or even Glasgow. They have a saying "When God made time, he made plenty of it!" Forget watches; hours and minutes are irrelevant. There is only "Good morning, good afternoon, good evening" with a lot of chatting in between. Shops often open late and are closed for lunch. In Tobermory, the gallery owner often wanders off to the pub, leaving his gallery open but unattended. One local summed it up best, saying, "We want to work but not too much."

The minor film classic *Local Hero* caught the pace of things to perfection. A young American city slicker flies over to a Highland coastal village in an attempt to buy the area from the locals for his company who want to drill the coastline for oil. He falls in love with the place, and when his boss arrives, he does too. The happy ending is that the place settles back down to its old quiet ways, to the joy and delight of everyone, especially the filmgoer.

177

The village shop is a lifeline to the more isolated Highlands communities.

Crime is also hardly an issue up north. Outside of the towns everyone leaves their cars and front doors open. Vandalism is almost unheard of and if there is any trouble it is usually drink-related and quickly sorted out the next morning.

Children

Youngsters benefit most from this laid-back environment. After a series of high-profile murder and sex abuse cases involving children in Britain over the past 20 years, parents keep an increasingly tight rein over their offspring. Whether this tendency not to let children out without close supervision is prudent or paranoid is debatable, but the end result is children are becoming dependent on television and computer games for entertainment.

In the Highlands, children run free. They can generally play outdoors and occupy themselves, with no greater worry than the occasional grazed knee. The big open country of the far North becomes a limitless playground for kids and their wild imaginations.

I remember, between bruising chases and cap gun fights, spending whole days in and around rock pools. Those tiny microcosms of oceans swept up and marooned amongst high rocks between tides offered us limitless fascination. Rather than learning about sharp edges and corners in concrete playgrounds, we studied starfish, sea anemones, and a hermit crab's slithering escape from under an upturned rock.

Of course the country can become a place of boredom and entrapment once children become teenagers looking for some action. Many of the young people who live in the Highlands today have a tough time of it. Often poor education in schools keeps them from building a bright future elsewhere while limited work prospects means they are frustrated and restless at home. The effect is demoralising, and can lead to a gradual slide into depression, and drink or drug abuse.

In one small village, one of the most scenic holiday destinations in the Highlands, the teenagers spend much of their time racing each other in souped-up cars. The talk in the bar is of their speeding antics and how they avoid the police on the slippery roads. It's as though the faster they go the sooner they will magically reach warp speed and escape to the thrills of modern big city life. While many go to the Highlands in search of the comfort of the natural world, these lads dream of going clubbing in Glasgow or London.

"There are two types of people in this village," says Tony, nicknamed the "balaclava," a shifty 16-year-old with a shocking fringe of black hair, "those who drink and those who smoke". Tony and his friends smoke grass like there's no tomorrow and boast of their experiences on the local hallucinogenic mushrooms. Some may get away to Australia, America or down south. Others like Tony seem to know they'll probably never leave and at the age of 16 carry this intuition like a life sentence. But even those who leave for the city life and never return treasure their memories of a childhood of relative simplicity and innocence.

My father has lived abroad since he went to university in Canada in the 1960s. He has no regrets about leaving the Highlands but once told me he can close his eyes and visualise every nook and cranny of the house he lived in as a child. He still walks through it in dreams, hearing the give of every window and door in the building.

THE DOWNSIDE

So life in the Highlands sounds idyllic after a visit in mid-summer, and seems to confirm all your wildest dreams of a romantic retreat. Suddenly the hills seem alive with the sound of music and you are ready to up sticks and move there tomorrow.

Only it's best to pause here before booking that one-way ticket to Inverness. The Highlands can be all that you dreamed of, but as you have read above, no place on earth is without its dark side and difficulties. It's important to ponder the downside of life in the Highlands, for like all new destinations, the grass may seem greener, but once you get there the reality can be bitter as well as sweet.

For a start you may well land in a village with a dusty kilt, a few key phrases like "...ay tis a fair crack," and all the best intentions in the world but you will still have to get the nod of approval from the villagers. Becoming an accepted member of a small community can be rather tricky.

An outsider's reception in a community depends on his or her commitment. If they are prepared to live there full-time and make a go of it they will probably find a higher degree of acceptance. However if you are looking to buy a house as a summer retreat from city life, expect a frostier welcome. Few newcomers are truly accepted until they have survived a couple of winters and proved to the local people that they are adaptable and aren't just decadent "sassenachs" or southerners.

Frustration is understandable if houses stand empty during the winter and the demand for holiday homes has artificially pushed up the property market in the area. This makes it harder for young local people to buy their first home and can turn communities into ghost villages for nine months of the year, with the local shop and post office closed for lack of customers.

A new resident's reception also depends on where they choose to settle. The further south you are in the Highlands, the more recent settlers there are, and the easier it is to be part of a mixed community. In popular destinations like the Island of Mull, hearing a local accent can be as rare as seeing the extraordinarily shy sea otter. You almost need a guide to spot one.

Moving into smaller communities further north, particularly in the islands, is much harder. Communities can be tight-lipped and closed, incomers tolerated but seldom welcomed. The feeling against English people in particular still runs high in areas where the historical memory of treatment at the hands of Cumberland's men after the Battle of Culloden is still amazingly fresh. In some west coast communities, only Gaelic is spoken to settlers and tourists alike. It's a big test of a newcomer's ability to adapt, even the Highlands and Islands' Tourist Board often answer the telephone in Gaelic.

Finding work in the northern Highlands can be difficult if you don't speak Gaelic. Alison Gill tried living in Lewis for 18 months but the whole time she was there job hunting, she didn't get a single reply to any of her applications. "One girl found work in the council and it was a front page scandal in the local paper that she came from Glasgow, even though she was originally born on Lewis and has recently moved back," Alison told me.

It can also be hard to adapt to areas where the Free Church still has a firm grip. The Free Church is a peculiarly Scottish form of Presbyterianism, closer to Calvinism in its Puritan zeal. Its control over public life is waning but in some communities the Sabbath is still strictly observed.

Sunday is sacred to the Free Church. Called the Sabbath, it is a day of rest in respect for God's work. A day of rest means more than just not going to work, a tradition common to the whole Christian world.

You can't garden, book into a hotel, or even put your washing out. Even the ferry doesn't run to Harris and Lewis on a Sunday.

Alison Gill was astonished when she first moved to Lewis. For a while she thought there was a funeral every Sunday because everyone was wandering around in stiff black suits and hats. She soon realised that they were just off to church. When it came to washing, even if she put out her sheets out on the line on a Monday morning she would get a visit from the minister to tell her off because she must have been washing them the night before.

One old tale sums up the severity of the Free Church and the strict observance of the Sabbath in some areas. In this particular fishing village, a fisherman, relatively new to the area, was out one Sunday morning on a rowing boat, checking his salmon nets. He fell and drowned ten metres from the shore in full view of the rest of the village, his waders tangled in the nets. Not a soul stepped out of their house to help him for he had broken an unwritten taboo by putting out his nets on a Sunday.

Stories like these bring back images from the classic horror flick, *The Wicker Man*. The story is of a young English detective drawn up to an isolated community to investigate a murder. After numerous sinister encounters with bearded fishermen he realises that the only murder is to be his own.

Loneliness is Such a Drag

In the Highlands there is a strong sense of isolation from the rest of the world. This is natural in a country where lines of communications are often tentative compared to the rest of western Europe. Often you can only reach the smaller communities by ferry or single-track road. Dealings with the outside world are reduced at times to the post runs by the red Royal Mail Land Rovers and visits from mobile bank vans, libraries, and chip vans.

In the village of Durness on the north coast, the nearest supermarket and swimming pool is 121 km (75 miles) away along single-track roads. Locals don't think twice about driving to Glasgow 483 km (300 miles) away to see a game of football.

I remember watching the science fiction series *Doctor Who* as a child on a snowy, crackling television. Only BBC 1 in black and white reached this remote peninsula in those days and the rest of Britain seemed worlds away.

Times have changed since then, now there are all kinds of mod cons in most homes, including colour television sets with multiple channels, mobile phones, and the Internet. Many are able to work from home with little more than a landline and a modem. There is even talk of setting up a virtual Internet University in the Highlands that will award degrees to students otherwise physically isolated by mountain and sea.

Gone are the days when the sturdy old red phone box on the edge of every village, lit by its single bulb, was a lifeline to a loved one or friend somewhere in the world beyond. Back then, the heavy click of the receiver at the end of the conversation would usher back a windy winter's night outside.

E-mail and mobile phones make little real difference if the ferry to the island still only runs a couple of times a day or the nearest sizeable town is a 161 km (100 miles) drive away. Communities are often still the isolated human settlements they have been for centuries. If you are used to living in a city, the novelty can wear off quickly. There are no coffee bars, bookshops, or cinemas and no more than one bar to drink in. The faces seldom change and any local news tends to spread like wild fire through dry woods.

Understandably, the froth of daily national public life makes little impact this far north. National newspapers make a meal of the latest political wrangling in Edinburgh or London, or the relative merits of one BBC breakfast show producer or another. Few in the Highlands care for this sort of news if it doesn't directly concern them. Local news covers different concerns. Take the following story picked out of the *Scotsman* as an example:

"The Shetland City council division of Receiver or Wrecks is refusing to clear up a large and decomposing sperm whale (40 tonnes) on the remote island of Vaila. The council claims the whale is the responsibility of the Scottish parliament. The dispute hangs over whether or not the whale is over 45 feet and therefore classed as the property of the crown and termed as "fish royal." It is to be measured and if found to be under 45 feet the responsibility for the rancid creature handed back to the council to clear up before it pollutes nearby mussel and salmon farms."

If there seems to be nothing of genuine importance to report on in the Highlands, there's usually something, or rather someone, to talk about all the same. Local trivia and tittle-tattle can become an all-consuming occupation in small communities where the art of gossiping is often skilled and sometimes bitter.

This can be incredibly frustrating for someone who has moved in from outside. For those used to the anonymity of the city, it can be a rude awakening to rural living to find their every action focused on and talked over by the locals.

Mary Underhill is an American who moved into a small community in the Highlands in the 1970s after she married a Scotsman. She loved the village and surrounding country but found the constant bickering exhausting. "There was constantly one storm in a tea cup or another and someone can be as sweet as pie to your face and then put in the knife behind your back," she said.

Personal disputes are continually aired and re-aired and old grudges rarely forgotten. If you live in the Highlands you will understand why the whole area is immersed in tall tales, superstitions, and heroic deeds. Small talk makes these villages worlds of living legend, where local heroes are revered for extraordinary feats of endurance, strength, or skill. Individual antics with drink, fighting, or speeding on the roads are exaggerated to become extraordinary "facts" that will be handed down from generation to generation.

Every village has them. The lad who can lift cars up with his bare hands or take the forestry road corners in a truck on two wheels. Or there's the man who's "heard tell" of having the fastest wit on the west coast. The Scots make great storytellers and the feats of one character or another are talked of from one village to the next.

Of course many of these folk are perfectly ordinary if you actually meet them. They've just become big fish in a small pond. Often it keeps them from leaving and you see the older characters propping up the village bars like old stags on the hill. It's hard to make a new beginning in Edinburgh or Glasgow without your local reputation to ride on.

ONE MORE FOR THE ROAD

There are countless stories and folk tales in the Highlands, and most of them originate from someone telling tales during a boozy night in some bar. The Scottish bar, common to most villages, is a focal point for socialising, especially on the long winter nights. Although traditionally an all-male domain, bars have in recent years become more popular with women as well. In this way they have improved by moving away from their rather macho atmosphere and taking in a broader sweep of village life.

The bar may hold community spirit together, a place where differences are lost in a pool of warm beer and hard spirits. However it is also the downfall of many. Drinking may be an integral part of Highland socialising but it leaves a trail of permanently sozzled men constantly propping up one bar or another. Every village has its drunks who spend all their earnings on staving off the next day's hangover with a few more for the road.

One old boy called Olrig lived in a small caravan behind our cottage. Most nights, even the freezing nights in winter, my Mother would watch him take his tortuous route back to the caravan along the track behind the cottage. Invariably tanked up from the pub, he would occasionally slip on the ice and, unable to right himself, would flail his limbs in the air like an overturned crab. She would speed out to help him get up before hypothermia set in. One night she grabbed his cane, ran inside, and hammered a few nails into one end of the cane to give the old man a bit more traction, and gave herself a break from her nightly vigil.

And I'm Not Looking Forward to the Journey Home

The enemies to life in the Highlands aren't just limited to boredom, gossiping and drink. There is also the weather and the dreaded midge to contend with. The weather in Scotland is amply touched on in other sections of this book so there is no sense in going on about it here. However, it is definitely a factor to take into consideration should you decide to stay in or even visit the Highlands. Talking of culture shock, there can be none harder that a first winter in the Highlands. You must be prepared with lots of indoor activities that you just love to do.

The climate up north may not always be that cold thanks to the Gulf Stream off the west coast, but although the summer days are gloriously long, "summer" is usually a euphemism for cold, wet, and windy weather. Winters are invariably wetter, colder, and very dark. The poet Alan Spence summed up the season in his native land with a Japanese haiku:

the sound of the rain
the sound of the rain
the sound of the rain

The comedian Billy Connolly spoke of meeting a tourist who said, "I went to Scotland and it rained." "Of course it rained!" was his reply. "What do you expect, the fucking Bahamas?"

Nights spent in around a peat fire in the dead of winter do hold their own charm. A quiet time of hibernation with oceans of time for storytelling, reading, or a lot of lovemaking, never did anybody any harm. As children, my brother and I had the entire Tolkien trilogy, *The Lord of the Rings*, read out loud to us by the fire one winter, twice for good measure.

Midge Attacks

And then there is Scotland's answer to the mosquito—the infamous midge—to contend with. So famous are these tiny torturers that whole books have been written about them, usually complete with illustrations of the "wee beasties'" antics in a tiny kilt and sporran. It makes you wonder how so much fuss can be made out of a tiny biting insect that only comes out between June and September.

But when you are actually caught in a black cloud of biting midges at dusk it all makes sense. They are maddening and so small that they get everywhere—into your ears, under your shirt, even crawling down to your scalp through your hair to get their fill. Their bite leaves little trace, but is like being touched by a thousand tiny fires, and the following itching can be pretty terrible too. By attacking in such huge numbers the effect is cumulatively horrible. Legend has it that when thieves were caught red-handed, they were tied and left naked overnight on a deserted road, to be driven mad by the midges.

One modern tale is enough of a warning to any unwitting traveller to the region. A friend's uncle, Colin Gladstone, is a farmer in Argyll on the west coast. One summer evening he came home from work to find he had left his bedroom window open and the room was thick with midges. Exhausted from work he fell into his bed and tried to get to sleep. As the midges fell on him in waves he got progressively more and more infuriated and desperate. In the middle of the night he snapped, jumped from his bed into his car still in his pyjamas and drove for 16 km (10 miles) into the hills where it was too windy for the midges. He opened the windows, and not willing to return to these unwelcomed guests in his bedroom he slept the rest of the night in the relative discomfort of his car.

The midge's relationship with the Scots is ambiguous. They are both reviled and tolerated, not that humans in Scotland have little choice when these insects thrive in their billions, breeding in the wet and boggy ground. The midges can make life miserable but they aren't around for most of the year and are widely credited for keeping the Highlands from being overrun by tourism in the summer months.

NORTHERN SOUL

Coming to the Highlands to live is a tough decision. So many people who bring passion and enthusiasm to the place find the sheen fades when the long winter of cold, dark, and boredom settles in. In many ways it's easier if you're born into it, when living in the Highlands isn't a lifestyle choice.

Still, everyone who lives or visits the Highlands can't help but be touched by the experience of this complex and wonderful place. The Highlands may not be the thriving, modern, urban heart of Scotland but it still has a magic that inhabits you while you're there and lingers on long after you have left it.

The Highlands are the ancient heart of Scotland and no arrival or departure to the country is complete without a trip up north. So where better to end this chapter than with a memory not of the Highlands, or the Lowlands, or even the popular tourist destinations along the Highlands' west coast but of Sutherland in the far north.

This seems a real frontier, like the end of the known world, and it never ceases to surprise me when I drive through it that such a land still exists in Europe. The mix of lake, moor, and cloud-wrapped mountains, brooding sentinel giants bound by the roaring seas, is like something out of Tolkien's *Lord of the Rings*. At its heart lies some dark secret, barely concealed by a thin Northern light. Even the bed-and-breakfast establishments are part of the same romance, with names like Rivendell and Saurian.

Outside of the towns and villages the only company is wind, sea, and stars. There are bars here covered with maps that chart the seas rather than the land, such is the ocean's dominance. On land, the place names—Cape Wrath, Loch Hope—indicate what a desperate act it must have been for those who first came to settle and invest in the place with their hopes and fears. Like Patagonia in South America it feels as though you're about to step off the end of the world here, as though you are at some lingering way station between life and the supernatural beyond.

It was dusk on Cape Wrath one evening in April. Lying on the shore that afternoon, the waves on the beach were so high the whole sea seemed set to engulf us. We had crawled out onto slippery black rocks to look at a seal colony, lolling around on a flinty outcrop at the tide edge. They seemed unassailable there in their fat rolls of glossy skin. Behind, the flipper of a porpoise rose above the sea's heavy swell, white-tipped by the wind.

The waves broke over this northern isle, cloaked in mist and spread with seaweed, and a pair of dark ravens flapped like loose canvas in the cavernous skies overhead. We turned up our collars and squinted out at an inscrutable horizon beyond: Iceland, the Arctic, a mirror of ourselves. This was Northern soul—Scotland at its most elemental, timeless, and unforgiving.

Chapter Ten

NUTS AND BOLTS

VISAS AND WORK PERMITS

Nationals from the European Economic Area

Nationals from the European Economic Area (EEA) are entitled to visit, live, or work in Great Britain. EEA countries are Austria, Belgium, Denmark, Finland, France, Germany, Greece, Iceland, Italy, Liechtenstein, Luxembourg, Netherlands, Norway, Portugal, Republic of Ireland, Spain, and Sweden.

If you are a European Union (EU) national you do not need to register with the police or get a residency permit. You only need to turn up with your passport, and if you intend to stay for longer than six months, prove that you are either working in the UK or have sufficient funds to support yourself. If you have family members who are not EEA nationals and who wish to come to the UK to live and work, they have to apply for an EEA family permit before they arrive.

After five years' residency in the UK, you can apply to stay indefinitely. To qualify, you have to have been working or financially self-supporting in the UK for at least four years and still have a right to residency. Applications take around 19 months to process.

Non-EEA Members

All citizens from European countries—except for Bulgaria, Romania, and all states of the former Soviet Union—can visit Britain for up to three months with nothing more than a passport. USA, Canadian, Australian, and New Zealand citizens can stay for up to six months. Citizens from all other countries require a visa to visit the UK, which is available from the British Consulate in the country of application. Some nationals, at immigration's discretion, also have to register within seven days of arrival at a local Police Registration Office.

Visitors can conduct business, provided that they are employed overseas. If you make frequent business trips to the UK, you can get a multiple entry visa, which normally lasts two years. This saves you the trouble of jumping hoops to get through immigration.

Visitors who are not citizens of European Union (EU) countries need a permit to work in the UK. This can be hard to get without backing from an established employer within Scotland. People between the ages of 17 and 27 can apply for a Working Holiday Maker Entry Certificate, which allows for two years casual work in the UK.

Commonwealth citizens who were born before January 1, 1983 and have at least one parent who is a British citizen, are considered British nationals. Commonwealth citizens with a British grandparent can also live and work in the UK for up to four years by claiming United Kingdom ancestry. If you are married to a British Citizen you can apply for British nationality provided it isn't a marriage of convenience for the sole purpose of gaining entry to the UK.

Students

Anyone can come to study in the UK provided they can prove that they are enrolled in a course of study involving a minimum of 15 hours organised daytime study per week. Prospective foreign students can also stay in the UK for up to six months, provided they can fund themselves as well as any course that they enrol in. Visa nationals still need to apply for a student or prospective student visa.

Foreign students are allowed to work for up to 20 hours a week part-time during term time but cannot take full-time vacancies. A foreign student's wife or husband and any children under 18 can join them. They are also entitled to work if the course of studies lasts for more than 12 months.

Asylum in the UK

Anyone who reaches the United Kingdom can claim asylum. The Home Office will then decide if they have a well-founded fear of persecution in the country that they are fleeing from. The process of assessing asylum seekers was speeded up in 1999, so an asylum seeker can expect to receive an answer within two months of his or her application.

During this time asylum seekers are given accommodation and a voucher food allowance, instead of cash. The voucher system has come under much criticism as asylum seekers can only spend their money in shops that accept vouchers. Organisations that work with asylum seekers feel this is demeaning and that the system denigrates and stigmatises asylum seekers by making them feel they are separate from the rest of society. The British government is currently reviewing the voucher system.

There are no official figures on the number of refugees in Scotland but under the government policy of dispersing asylum seekers out of the London area, numbers are on the rise. The highest concentrations of refugees are in Glasgow.

GETTING THERE

Most international flights fly into one of London's four airports: Gatwick, Heathrow, Luton, or Stansted. The airline companies British Airways, Go, Air UK, Ryanair, and Easy Jet offer the most frequent connections from London airports to either Glasgow's Preswick Airport or Edinburgh airport. Flights generally cost from £55 one way, but you can find deals for as little as £30 return. From Edinburgh and Glasgow you can fly on to Aberdeen, Inverness, or to another of Scotland's 17 internal airports. Internal flights are operated by British Airways Express.

There are several daily nonstop flights to Glasgow from New York, Chicago, and Boston in North America. Fares vary depending on the time of year. The low season is from mid-January to the end of February and then October through to November. The high season is from mid-May until the end of August.

Ever since the Vikings first landed in Scotland, links have been retained with Norway by sea. In June and August the Smyril line sails between Shetland, Norway, the Faeroe Islands, Iceland, and Denmark. A more direct route is from Bergen in Norway to Lerwick in Shetland and then on to Aberdeen with P&O Ferries. The crossing has a reputation for being a rough one.

Many tourists coming from mainland Europe prefer to take shorter crossings to the North of England and then drive to Scotland. North Sea ferries sail from Rotterdam and Zeebrugge to Hull. From there it's only a four-hour drive to Scotland. From Newcastle in the North of England it is also possible to sail to and from Bergen and Stavanger in Norway, Gothenburg, Amsterdam, or Hamburg. Further South, Stena Sealink, and P&O Ferries offer frequent connections between Dover and French ports but the drive north is considerably longer, taking up the best part of a day. To jump over to that other Celtic heartland, Ireland, there are two ferry services running from Scotland. P&O Ferries runs daily sailings from Stranraer to Belfast and European Ferries connects Larne with Cairnryan.

Trains

The guard at the tiny Highland station of Dalwhinnie swings his heavy green lantern and the old diesel train starts to pull away at a walking pace. It's night and the *Isle of Iona* sleeper from Inverness to London has a long, jolting way to go before it reaches the big city. It seems in no hurry, content to beetle on slowly south, a row of lights under a starless night.

Train travel holds a certain romance in Scotland. Locals and tourists alike are fond of routes like the overnight sleeper to Inverness or the stunning trip from Inverness to the Kyle of Lochalsh on the west coast.

In fact trains are so popular to some enthusiasts that you may see small men with beards and notepads at some station platforms, eagerly writing down the names and registrations of passing trains. They are an exclusive breed known as trainspotters—as far as I know, they are peculiar to Britain.

The train network in Scotland is not as extensive as it was before many of the smaller branch lines were closed in the mid-sixties. Areas of Scotland, such as the borders in the south and the far northwest coast are poorly connected.

The most popular routes are regular and efficient. For example trains leave every fifteen minutes between Edinburgh and Glasgow. With rail privatisation in the early nineties making the network profit-driven, routes to less popular destinations are being increasingly neglected and can often suffer delays.

A series of rail disasters in England—at Clapham in 1998, Paddington in 1999, and Hatfield in 2000—has also raised serious safety questions for the rail network. Urgent repairs to track, signalling, and the rolling stock will bring further disruption for passengers in the future.

Train information is available at the stations or on a central number (0345 484950). You can buy train tickets and reserve seats with cash or credit card either directly at the station or over the phone. As the network has been sold off to different private companies, you need to book over the phone from the company that operates the particular route that you are travelling on. The Great North Eastern Railway (GNER) travels between London, Edinburgh, and Inverness. Virgin trains travel between London and Glasgow, and Scotrail covers most train travel within Scotland.

Train fares in Scotland, and across Britain as a whole tend to be expensive compared to other European countries. For example, a standard return from Edinburgh or Glasgow to London—four hours of travel each way—costs around £80. That is only for standard accommodation, first class costs over £100. Most trains have one specifically designated smoking carriage.

It is possible to find cheaper fares. Travel on Fridays and peak holiday dates is always more expensive. There is the option of booking one week in advance for an Apex or two weeks in advance for a super Apex ticket. These fares give up to a third off on the standard ticket price. However you have to commit yourself to your travel dates in advance and the ticket is non-refundable if you wish to travel at another time.

If you are under 26 or a full-time student, it is well worth buying a student railcard. This is a rail pass that gives one third off all destinations. They cost £18 for a year and are available from any ticket office. You are required to show proof of age or that you are a full time student if you ask for one. There is a similar card for families and those over 60 also offering up to one third off rail travel. There are also central Scotland and Highland Rover tickets that offer deals for passengers who plan to tour around the country by train.

Buses and Post Vans

Bus travel is a considerably cheaper means for getting around Scotland, especially in the more isolated areas that can't be reached by train. A typical overnight return fare from London to Glasgow or Edinburgh is £30. Tickets and information are available directly from the bus stations.

National Express is the main operator between Scotland and England. The bus company Stagecoach also has extensive coverage within Scotland. Buses are considerably cheaper than train travel but tend to be more cramped and uncomfortable. A student discount card as well as concessionary rates for children is available.

Numerous backpacker tours offer flying visits into the Highlands in a minibus with food, accommodation, and a tour guide thrown in. Departing from Edinburgh or Glasgow, a typical three-day tour costs a very affordable £60. Running on very tight schedules, these tours can involve much more sitting in a crowded bus than actually exploring the Highlands.

In the Highlands, the smaller villages are most easily accessed by the post vans. These red station wagons or land rovers race from community to community, dropping off mail, messages and packages as they go. For a small fee you can take a ride in the back of one of them, provided your destination is on their route. The post van times are available from local post offices but you need to allow a good margin to pick one up either way. Due to the speed at which they negotiate the small winding roads they are often ahead of time.

Ferry

Ferry travel is more than a quaint way to see Scotland; it is an essential means of transport to and from the 130 inhabited islands scattered around the coast. The company Caledonian Macbrayne runs most of the routes, all of them with roll-on roll-off car ferries. The main exceptions are the routes from Scrabster to Orkney and Aberdeen to the Shetland Isles, which are operated by P&O.

Ferry transport isn't cheap. The best option, if you plan to jump from island to island, is to buy an Island Hopscotch or Island Rover ticket, which offers multiple sailings over a set period of time at an economy price. It is advisable to reserve a place ahead of time during the peak period (April-October) if you are taking a car. During the winter months, many run limited services and some non-essential routes dry up altogether.

Hitching

Scotland has a strong car culture and hitching isn't that common when most have their own transport. However it is a common sight to see bedraggled walkers in the summer in the Highlands, desperately trying to hitch a ride with their mountainous backpacks filled with mouldy clothes.

To hitch a ride, find a suitable lay-by and stand looking mournful and harmless with your thumb up and the rest of your hand closed in a fist. It helps to write your destination on a big piece of card. Be prepared for a wait, there is little charity on the roads in Scotland. Hitch at your own risk—it is not safe for women to hitch alone.

Around Town

Taxis are plentiful in all of the main cities. The safest and most reliable are the black cabs, with their bright orange *Taxi* sign on the front of the roof. When the light is switched off, it means the taxi is occupied.

Taxis are expensive. A short trip across town will start at an average of £5. Tipping is not necessary in Scotland but is always appreciated, especially if the driver takes the time to help you with you baggage. Buses are much cheaper (from 50 pence a ride) but their erratic frequency and speed and can be bewildering.

Glasgow has its very own Metro system, known as the underground. It is a modest affair compared to the jumble of lines that crisscross under London, but no less effective. For 80 pence you can travel the length of the city, from north to south and east to west.

The simplest way to get around is on foot. With the exception of Glasgow which is too large to stroll around easily, cities in Scotland are small enough to explore on foot. A-Z maps found in most bookshops and newsagents make direction finding relatively easy and if you're lost, there is always a local to help you out. The Scottish love to give directions, occasionally walking with you some of the way to make sure you're on the right track.

DRIVING IN SCOTLAND

Britain drives on the left. That includes Scotland, Wales, Northern Ireland, and England, so beware if you are used to driving on the right. It's easier not to get confused if you drive a British car with the steering wheel on the right-hand side.

There is a peculiar country code if you are driving in the Highlands. Much of this remote country is covered with single-track roads with passing places, meaning you can't pass an oncoming vehicle without one of you pulling over. It also makes overtaking impossible and long queues can form behind slow-moving cars and caravans. Passing places are also there for slow cars to pull in for cars behind to overtake. Pulling over to let people pass isn't a law but it is the custom, and if ignored can infuriate fast-moving locals who know the roads.

If someone pulls over to let you by, it is important to thank them either with a raised hand or a flash of your lights. If one hand is on the gear stick and the other on the wheel, just lift your index finger up off the wheel to signal your appreciation.

Beware of getting caught short without any petrol. In the Highlands, petrol stations can get pretty sparse. In the more isolated areas, some of the smaller pumps can also be closed on Sundays. There is nothing worse than spending an afternoon driving with your eyes fixed on the petrol gauge rather than the surrounding scenery.

Car hire is relatively affordable in Scotland. You can hire a car for as little as £12 a day with nothing more than a valid UK or International driving licence and your credit card details. If you damage the hire car or van on your travels, you will be obliged by all hire companies to pay a part of the damages. This varies between £100 and £250; any more is covered by their insurance. The bigger companies, such as Arnold Clark, have centres across Scotland, so if you wish you can pick up a car in Glasgow and drop it off in Inverness.

Driving Licence

You can get a British driving licence from the age of 17 by passing a driving test at a local test centre. Driving tests are notoriously rigorous in Britain and involve both a practical test of driving skills on the road and a written test of driving rules and regulations.

While learning to drive, you are allowed to brave the open road provided you have a provisional licence, are insured, and have someone with a full licence in the passenger seat at all times. An "L" plate must be attached to the front and back of the vehicle to show you are still learning to drive.

Driving instructors offer courses of tuition running up to the test day for around £25 an hour. With the advent of the virtual world of computer technology, some driving tuition centres also offer virtual driving simulation for a fraction of the price of normal lessons.

By law you are required to update the address on your driving licence if you move house. This is a simple affair that involves filling out part of the licence and sending it off to be changed. The process takes around 10 days, during which time you can continue driving. If you are caught with an old address on your licence, you are liable for a heavy fine. Driving licences are valid right up until the age of 70, when it is required to have a sight test to keep driving on the road.

Buying into the Car Culture

Buying a car or motorbike anywhere in the world can be a risky business, especially if it's second hand. Buying a car new from a showroom or second hand from a dealer is relatively straightforward as they all come with a guarantee that covers hidden problems.

The riskiest but cheapest option is to buy directly from the last owner. Cars and motorbikes are advertised in a number of magazines, the biggest ones being *Auto Trader* and *Supermarket*. To avoid paying too much for a second hand car the magazine *Parker's Used Car Guide* gives an accurate and up-to-date guide on how much you can expect to pay for a particular model and age.

It is worth having a local mechanic look at a second-hand car before you commit. This can be arranged at a local garage for a fee, or the Automobile Association (AA) will send out one of their mechanics to have a look for around £160. Once you have bought a vehicle, it needs to be registered in your name. The previous owner will have the vehicle registration document, to which you add your details, and send it off to the Vehicle Registration Centre in Swansea.

All vehicles need to have a valid road tax certificate. Road tax varies depending on the type and size of the vehicle. Motorcycles cost between £15 and £40 for a year. Cars which have smaller engines (less than 1,500 cc) pay £100, anything over costs £155 a year. It is also possible to pay for road tax every six months. It is illegal to have a car on the road (even parked) with an out-of-date tax disk.

To buy a road tax certificate, you have to show a valid Ministry of Transport (MOT) certificate and insurance policy for the vehicle. The MOT test is carried out yearly on all vehicles by garages and MOT centres. The test is an evaluation of the general roadworthiness of the vehicle. If the vehicle fails on any count, relevant repairs need to be carried out before the certificate can be issued.

Insurance policies can be bought over the phone from any number of companies or brokers listed in the yellow pages. There are two types of policies. Third party fire and theft will cover any damage to other vehicles if you are in an accident. It will also pay for the vehicle if it is stolen or suffers fire damage. Fully comprehensive, which is generally more expensive, also covers any damage to your own vehicle, including bumps or accidents which are your own fault. Insurance cover starts from around £250.

If you are involved in an accident with another vehicle it is important to exchange vehicle licence plate numbers and names and addresses with the other driver. The details of paying for damages are then negotiated between each driver's insurance company. If you are in a crash and the other driver tries to make a getaway, make a note of their licence plate and the police can track them down.

It is worth becoming a member of a breakdown and recovery service in case you get stranded on a roadside. For a one-off payment of around £100 a year you can call up for on-the-spot roadside repair or transport to the nearest garage if the problem can't be patched up there and then. The biggest companies with nationwide coverage are the RAC (0800 887766) and the AA (0800 828282).

THE COLOUR OF MONEY

Anyone can open a bank account in Britain provided they can show proof of identity and proof of address. Proof of identity can be a passport, driving licence, photo identity card, pension or benefit book or birth certificate. Proof of address can be a current household bill (gas, electricity, telephone, water, and council tax) or another official document which shows your name and address, such as a bank or credit card statement.

Banks, building societies, and the post office offer a wide range of different types of accounts with varying degrees of interest, so it is well worth looking around before committing. Most banks also offer credit cards.

With the introduction of direct banking in Britain it is becoming easier to manage an account. You can now make a phone call or log onto the Internet to pay bills, check balances, and order chequebooks. Although this is all very neat it does threaten thousands of branch office jobs, which may no longer be needed to help deal with customer accounts and inquiries.

Cash machines are the most common way to withdraw money in Scotland. Most banks and building societies have cash dispensing machines outside their offices. Cash machines are well networked and it is possible to take out money and check your account from most bank and building society machines, regardless of whether or not you bank with them. Some cash tellers will charge up to £2 a transaction for this service.

While most currencies in Europe are now standardised under the euro, Britain is still reluctant to join. The pound sterling currency—divided into 100 pence—is the same in Northern Ireland, Wales, England, and Scotland, although the designs on the coins and notes can differ.

Coins are straightforward, as the distinctive sizes for differing denominations don't vary. There are £2 and £1 coins and then 50p, 20p, 10p, 5p, 2p, and 1p coins. Scottish notes printed by the Royal Bank of Scotland, the Bank of Scotland, and the Clydesdale bank are very distinctive, proudly sporting the heads of famous entrepreneurial Scottish figures. Notes printed from the Bank of England, Scotland, or Northern Ireland are also legal tender throughout the British Isles.

Notes come in denominations of £100, £50, £10, and £5. Scotland is unique in having a £1 note, which has long since been discontinued elsewhere in the British Isles.

POST

The Royal Mail, one of the few remaining public services in Britain, is fast and efficient. Mail is delivered to the door, seldom lost, and is easy to post from the multitude of little red boxes that have become something of a trade mark for the British Isles.

When addressing mail it's important to follow a clear order:
- Addressee's name
- Building number or name
- Street name (if there is one)
- Locality name (if there is one)
- Post town (in capital letters)
- Postcode (in capital letters)

The postcode should always be on a separate line at the end of the address. If you don't know the postcode call the enquiry line on 08457 111222 or visit *Postcodes Online* at http://www.royalmail.co.uk. It is also recommended to put the return address on the back of mail; if it can't be delivered, Royal Mail will return it for free.

Stamps are bought in booklets of up to £5 in most newsagents or individually from post offices. First-class stamps cost 27p for a letter under 60 grams and generally reach their destination the next day anywhere in the British Isles. A second-class stamp for a postcard or letter costs 19p and takes around three working days to arrive. Heavier letters and packages cost more depending on their weight.

There are a number of options to guarantee delivery. For an extra 63p, mail can be sent recorded, which means that the sender is given a receipt on posting and the letter or package is signed for on delivery. For an additional fee starting at £3.50, mail is guaranteed to be delivered the next day, provided it is sent before noon. To check that a recorded item has arrived, call 08459 272100 or go to the Royal Mail's website at http://www.royalmail.co.uk.

Letters up to 20g and postcards to the whole of Europe cost 36p. Mail sent abroad can be sent by surface mail or, for a little more money but quicker delivery time, by airmail. All mail sent by air needs an airmail sticker, or "PAR AVION—BY AIRMAIL," written on the top left hand corner of the letter or package. British Mail aims to deliver letters to Western Europe in two days following the day of posting and to countries outside of Europe in 4 days. Most packages containing goods that are sent outside of the EU need a customs label, available from post offices.

If you do not wish to have mail delivered directly to your home, you can arrange to have a PO Box set up. This is an alternative address where post is held until you pick it up at your local post office (to apply call 08457 950950). If you move, you can also arrange to have mail sent on to a new address in the UK, or sent abroad via airmail, for up to two years.

CRIME

Scotland is a relatively law abiding and peaceful place. Although there is a rise in gangland style shootings in urban areas across Britain, the country does not have a gun culture and the police still walk the streets with little more than a baton and handcuffs. Stabproof vests and a chemical spray to ward off aggressors is to be introduced as standard for the police force but the days of seeing coppers or bobbies on the streets with sidearms is still a long way off.

Simple precautions are the best way to ward off petty crime in Scotland. Lock up your vehicle, room, or house when you leave it and don't leave valuable possessions in the car untended. Avoid dark and unlit places in urban areas at night and be aware of who is around you when you take money out of a cash machine somewhere quiet. If someone threatens you for money, give it to them, they aren't joking.

More serious crimes such as rape, assault, or murder are not common in Scotland. Most of the violence is domestic, or fights between young men—and occasionally women—late at night with a few drinks inside them. Like anywhere else in the world, women should take care if they are on their own in a town or city late at night. The further north you go into the Scottish Highlands, the safer it gets.

If you have been the victim of violence, call the police immediately on free phone 999 to report it. Officers will be sent out to investigate and there is more of a chance of catching the perpetrators than by finding a police station to report it. All other inquiries should be made at police stations.

THE WELFARE STATE

The welfare state, set up under the Liberal prime-minister Lloyd George at the beginning of the last century aimed to provide state support for its citizens from the cradle to the grave. Over sixty years on, the welfare state is still in place. For all the system's bureaucracy and funding shortages—and there is plenty of both—it still provides a vital service to those who need it.

Health care is largely free for everyone and additional support is available for people who are struggling to keep their heads above water financially. This includes everyone from the unemployed to disabled people, pensioners, families, and children. Help can come in many forms including cash payments, tax credit, housing, home help for the elderly, and legal aid.

Healthcare and other state benefits, also known as social security, are available to anyone who is from a member country of the European Union (EU). Some countries outside of the EU also have reciprocal agreements with the UK. For example Iceland, Liechtenstein, and Norway are considered members of the EU when it comes to cash benefits.

People outside the EU are also eligible for social security if they are a refugee or a dependant of the widow or widower of anyone who was eligible. You cannot claim benefits if you are a full-time student. For specific information on benefits and related health care cover contact:

Benefits Agency
Department of Social Security
Pensions and Overseas Benefit
Directorate
Newcastle on Tyne
NE98 1BA
Tel: 0191 2187777
Fax: 0191 2187293

Healthcare

Healthcare under the National Health Service (NHS) is free for anyone who is eligible. The first port of call is the local doctor or General Practitioner (known as a GP). To be assigned a doctor you need to register with a health centre or doctor's surgery in the area. You only need to show that your permanent address is within that health centre's boundaries.

An appointment will then be made for you to have a general check up with your GP, after which you can make an appointment with him or her whenever you wish. After you have been registered you can visit any health centre in the country for a temporary visit if needed. Visiting a doctor is free but prescriptions have to be bought and paid for at a pharmacy. If an ailment or injury needs further attention, a doctor will refer you to the appropriate specialist or hospital.

Health centres have emergency doctors available 24 hours a day for urgent cases. Most hospitals have an accident and emergency department that anyone can visit without an appointment if they need urgent treatment. There are often long waiting lists for non-urgent cases. In recent years, a number of private health care companies have set up shop, offering prompt treatments at a price.

There is also a burgeoning interest in alternative medicines in recent years. With doctors unable to give much time to their patients together with new age movements concerned with more holistic treatments, many are turning to alternative therapies. It's now possible to find treatments such as acupuncture, homoeopathy, herbal medicine, and osteopathy across Scotland. Most of these treatments are not funded by the NHS and must be paid for. Although a few GPs are willing to recommend these treatments to patients, they are unable to make a formal referral to anyone who isn't also a registered medical doctor.

Free dental care is also available to unemployed people on benefits. However, it is increasingly difficult to find dental practices that offer these services as many of them have become privatised.

Other State Benefits

To claim state benefits you need a National Insurance number. If you do not already have a national insurance number, make an appointment at the local social security office. You need to bring proof of identity, such as a passport or driving licence. National Insurance numbers take between three and six weeks to be assigned. During this time any claims can be backdated but no benefits payment will be made until the National Insurance number comes through.

You may also have to take a habitual residency test to establish that you are living long-term in the country. This is largely to prevent foreign students from coming over to Britain and claiming benefit for a few months in the summer.

Job Centres, scattered across the country, process claims and advertise work. There is a vast array of benefits forms on offer and claims are processed depending on individual circumstances.

The most common benefit is the job seekers' allowance, a weekly allowance of £55 a week to support people who are unemployed and looking for work. To qualify, you have to be available for work at any time and be willing to work part- or full-time.

People unemployed for the longer term, (six months or more for young people between the ages of 18 and 24 and over two years for those aged 25 or over), come under the "New Deal." Introduced under the Prime Minister Tony Blair in 1998, the "New Deal" offers support with education and training, as well as greater pressure to find work.

If you are unemployed, or earn less than £60 a week you can also claim housing benefit. Housing benefit will pay the rent for you. There is currently a three- to six-month backlog on claims. Although the rent money is backdated to when you first made a claim, many landlords prefer not to wait and will not accept tenants who wish to claim housing benefit.

EDUCATION

There is no integrated childcare system in Scotland. Children under five years of age have nursery day places provided by social services or nursery schools, provided by the Education Department for children aged three or over. Additional support is available from pre-school play groups. Organised and coordinated by the Scottish Pre-school Play Group Association, parents take turns to look after each other's children.

Children start formal education at the age of four or five at primary school. Primary school runs for seven years until they reach high school. At high school level, those parents who can afford it will decide whether or not to send their children to state school, or to have them educated privately.

Private schools, often confusingly called public schools, offer more intensive tuition, better facilities and can be mixed or single sex. Private boarding schools take children off parent's hands completely during term time, providing accommodation and full catering on site. Gordonstoun, situated near Elgin in the Highlands, is a favoured choice for the Royals: Prince Charles and his father both studied there. Boarding schools are also famed for their obsession with punishing sports such as rugby and endemic bullying between students (euphemistically called fagging). All state schools are day schools.

There is more to offer in the fee-paying world than traditional public schools, or schools such as Gordonstoun. Rudolf Steiner's educational system was founded in 1919 to encourage children's personal development rather than pushing them through a rigid education system. Its popularity is growing in Scotland, and there are currently four schools in the country, charging around £1,000 per child each term. Scottish MSP's are considering following the example of Denmark, Norway, and Germany to fund Steiner schools publicly, making them part of the maintained school sector.

School qualifications are the same regardless of what school you send your children to. After four years of high school or secondary school, students, usually when they are fifteen or sixteen years old, sit for their standard grade exams (usually seven exams). After this they are free to leave, or study for one more year and sit for an average of five Highers. Entrance into higher education is dependent on exam results from the Highers.

The Scottish system differs from the English high school exams, which starts with GCSE's at standard grade levels and ends with the Highers equivalent of GCE Advanced levels. Advanced levels, also known as A levels, last two years rather than one and take on fewer subjects (usually three) in greater depth. A few of the privately run schools in Scotland offer the English system. Confusing as all of this sounds, it makes no substantive difference when it comes to higher education. Institutes of higher education within Great Britain and abroad accept both qualifications.

Around 50% of the 60,000 school leavers in Scotland go on to some form of further education. There is no shortage of choice: There are 23 Higher Education Institutes in Scotland. Fourteen of these institutes are universities (including the Open University) and the remainder are technical colleges which offer a wide variety of vocational courses and training.

University degree courses last a year longer in Scotland than in England—four years on average rather than three. Students can choose to finish after three years, if they wish, and be awarded a General degree. If they go the full course, they come out with a Masters with Honours. More than 38,000 students graduate every year from university.

The Scottish education system is highly valued both within Britain and abroad, drawing many foreign students to its shores. Many are attracted by the prestige of particular university faculties. For example Herriot Watt has been famed for centuries for its excellence in medicine. So keen was the demand for bodies for autopsies and medical research in the 19th century that graves were frequently robbed in Edinburgh to keep up the supply. The gruesome tale of William Burke and William Hare's search for fresh specimens comes straight out of the darker days of scientific inquiry in Edinburgh.

William Burke and William Hare are the world's most notorious body-snatchers. Over a 12-month period from 1827–1828, they murdered over a dozen people in Edinburgh and sold their corpses to a local anatomy school desperate for fresh bodies to dissect. When they were finally tracked down and caught by the police, Hare famously gave evidence against Burke in exchange for his own freedom. Burke swung from the gallows and Hare disappeared, never to be seen again.

Strathclyde University has one of the largest engineering facilities in the UK, with around 3,000 full-time students. The arts are also well represented. Glasgow University is famed for its art courses as well as the stunning building designed by Charles Mackintosh that houses them. The art department at Dundee University is also highly regarded.

These are just a few of the many examples of fine Scottish universities. Rebecca Castro from Chile who has just finished a Masters Degree in Computer Science from Napier University hopes to find a good job in the computer industry in the next few months. "The tuition is excellent and I'm confident that I can find work here or abroad with little problem," she told me.

Mind you, with university courses costing foreign students anything from £7,000 a year for tuition alone, the standard of education needs to be pretty high.

Unlike many countries, most students study away from home after they have finished high school. Universities often offer shared accommodation in halls of residence for the first year or for post-graduate students, but most opt for shared squalor in a cheap flat.

This tradition may be set to change. British university students used to be well looked after with state grants and free tuition. In recent years however, the grants have been replaced by long-term loans and students in Scotland now have to pay £2,000 toward their tuition fees after they have completed their course as opposed to £3,000 up front in England.

As a result many students are opting to study from home to keep costs down. Perhaps the new University of the Highlands and Islands (UHI), which aims to link students studying from home with different educational institutions via the Internet, is the sign of things to come.

A ROOF FOR THE NIGHT

Temporary accommodation is as varied as it is plentiful in Scotland. At the top of the range there is the country's ubiquitous trademark, the historic castle. No longer damp and miserable sites of siege and starvation, many castles these days offer luxury accommodation for the few that can afford it.

If you find a castle is too ostentatious—or expensive—a good second option is an old shooting lodge. Many of these have been converted into hotels, giving a glance at a whole lifestyle as well as a warmish bed for the night. But lodges are often draughty and poorly heated, so bring plenty of warm clothing.

Sporting lodges are not for the fainthearted. Expect to dine surrounded by the stuffed animal trophies of wild beasts that made it to the dinner table. Most of these lodges offer fishing and shooting in as a package and are usually booked for weeks at a time by big groups during the summer.

Hotels and inns are common across Scotland and serve a double function. They provide accommodation for tourists in the country at reasonable prices ranging from £20–£40 on average. They often also house the local bar for residents in the off season. So if you are looking for a slice of reality, check out the hotel bar, often tucked away from the rest of the hotel. The stained tartan carpet, scuffed up pool table, and assortment of rough-looking characters around the bar can seem intimidating at first. But if you take the time for a few drinks you'll have a great night and learn more about Scotland than you would from any number of guidebooks.

Next in line is the good old bed and breakfast, known as a B&B. B&Bs are a unique British institution and another good way of meeting locals while supporting the local economy. A bed and breakfast is a home that is owned privately and opened to travellers to stay in spare rooms. For as little as £12 a night per person, you can expect to get a comfortable room and feast on a legendary cooked breakfast in the morning.

You can't miss bed-and-breakfast establishments, drive into Fort William, and there is a sign in front of every other house offering rooms, all in fierce competition with their neighbours. The only downside is that in a small house, you may feel like you are invading the family's personal space and end up tiptoeing around on eggshells, desperately trying to be invisible.

Youth hostels are traditionally the best budget option for putting a roof over your head for a night. Despite their name, they are open to anyone of any age, offering a bunk bed in a shared, single-sex dorm.

The Scottish Youth Hostelling Association (SYHA) is the biggest organisation that runs hostels. Their brochure, available in any tourist information office, details an impressive array of settings. Many of their hostels are old country houses set in beautiful countryside. Their flagship, Carbisdale Castle in Sutherland, has 197 beds and a collection of the finest privately owned Italian marble statues in Britain.

The SYHA has gone a little more upmarket in recent years, and prices for a night are now comparable to bed-and-breakfasts (between £9 and £15). However, they do offer kitchen facilities, a television lounge, breakfast, and plenty of information on various outdoor activities. Other independent youth hostels tend to be cheaper.

For many who visit Scotland, particularly the Highlands, comfort is an unwanted luxury. Hardened hillwalkers and climbers expect adversity, and sleeping on a roll mat on boggy ground somehow adds to the authenticity of the experience. Enter the camper's world, where there is no finer pleasure than a can of baked beans with cheese heated up on the primer gas stove after a long day's walk.

Campsites are plentiful, offering parking, showers and toilets for no more than a few pounds a night. Once in the Highlands it is not always necessary to find a campsite. With ample free space to choose from, you can often pitch a tent anywhere as long as you are out of sight of the road and the local farmer. As long as you don't leave any litter or end up burning down the local woods, most locals will turn a blind eye.

A *bothy* is a good way station on a rain-blown evening with failing light, especially when you're faced with the prospect of spending a restless night under canvas. Bothies are unique public spaces that hold something of the open free spirit of the Highlands. No more that an empty cottage with a few beds and a stone hearth, they are open to anyone who happens to be passing and needs shelter. Bothies are free to stay in and rely on the good will of walkers to leave them tidy with the fire set and perhaps some spare food for the next travellers.

You can't get to a bothy by car; they are scattered across the most inhospitable areas of the Highlands and have undoubtedly saved countless people who would have otherwise perished in a sudden blizzard. Most bothies in Scotland have been meticulously marked on Ordnance Survey maps, so they shouldn't be too hard to find.

The tatty visitor's books found in bothies tell countless tales of long walks and tall tales told round the fire in years past. One of the most chilling legends comes out of Barrisdale on the isolated Knoydart peninsula.

Legend has it that a giant pterodactyl-like flying beast frequents the valley and occasionally dines on passing travellers. On windy nights there are numerous stories of the Barrisdale Beast descending onto the roof of the bothy in the valley, and clawing at it to get at the terrified walkers within.

If all else fails there is always a night under the stars, not as impossible a prospect as it may seem in Scotland. My most memorable night in the great outdoors was spent in a sleeping bag on the shores of Loch Awe. A midnight sky cleared to put on a brilliant show of Northern lights. Sheets of shimmering colour and cartwheels of fairy lights lit up the lake in front. I fell asleep trying to imagine how people saw those lights before they were explained away by scientific reasoning; they must have seemed to be a message from somebody's gods. We woke the next morning to a grey leaden sky and frost on our sleeping bags. The magic had definitely moved on.

Rented Accommodation

Rooms, flats, and houses for let are advertised in local papers and most estate agents. It is also worthwhile going to the area that you would like to live in and looking at the notice boards of newsagents and cafés. This is the quickest and easiest way of finding rooms in shared flats or houses. Landlords may ask for bank and personal references before considering you as a tenant.

Once you have agreed to rent a place, you will be expected to pay the landlord or landlady the first month's rent in advance as well as a deposit. The deposit is generally two times the monthly rent, but this can vary. The deposit is returnable when you leave, provided that you have not damaged the property and are up to date with your rent. The landlord is responsible for repairing general wear and tear on a property, such as broken electrical appliances.

Unscrupulous landlords often withhold deposits on false pretexts, such as claiming that a tenant was responsible for damages made before they arrived. I have even heard of one case where the landlord claimed a tenant had stolen an entire sofa that was never there in the first place. Make sure your landlord gives you an inventory of the contents when you move in and check that everything on the list is there. It is also worth pointing out, or even photographing any existing damage so that you aren't made to pay for it when you leave.

You will also have to sign a tenancy agreement with the landlord. Make sure that you read this carefully before you sign your life away, landlords can sneak in unreasonable demands. A standard tenancy agreement is for one year, but this sometimes includes a get-out clause for the tenant requiring a month's notice should you need to leave early.

Renting a place in Scotland can be expensive. There is the Government's community charge tax to pay, which varies depending on the value of the property but runs into hundreds of pounds a year. Properties occupied by full-time students are not subject to community charge. However, if one or more of the occupants is not a student, the tax is levied regardless.

Water, electricity, and gas bills are sent out quarterly. If you don't pay the first bill, you will be first sent a reminder and then finally a red reminder. This gives you seven days to pay up or face credit black listing, legal action, and having your supply disconnected. Discounts are sometimes given if you pay your bills promptly. All televisions require television licences, an annual fee of around £100. If you don't pay your television licence, you may get fined £1,000.

Bills are most commonly paid by sending a cheque in the post. However a more convenient method is direct debit, where an agreed amount of money is taken directly out of your bank account on a set date each month. Direct debit is now used to pay for everything from bills and rent to subscriptions, insurance, and contact lenses.

TELEPHONES

Gone are the days when a whole community would be connected into one local operator. In the Sound of Sleat in the south of the Isle of Skye, one local resident told me how sixty years ago, she used to pick up the phone and talk directly to the operator, who would then put her through to the house she was calling. The only problem was that the whole community could quietly pick up their receivers and listen into the conversation. Everything said over the phone became public knowledge.

British Telecom (BT), then the state monopoly holder on telecommunications, has become considerably more sophisticated. Now an impressive array of cordless phones, fax phones, itemised bills, phone cards and answer services are on offer. Since becoming privatised, BT now has a whole field of competitors so do shop around. Some of these companies, such as Planet Talk, offer extremely cheap international rates.

Mobile phones have become the latest 21st century icon for being cool across Britain. Having a mobile gives instant kudos; it says, "I'm young, mobile, and can have noisy telephone conversations in public places." Getting a good deal on a mobile phone is relatively easy as the terrestrial phone companies are in hot competition with the mobile phone companies, which in turn are in hot competition with each other.

Number Crunching

Business numbers are advertised in the hefty *Yellow Pages*, delivered free to all. Private numbers and businesses are listed in local directories called *The Phone Book*. This blue book also includes information on dialling codes and the numbers of essential services. Dial 192 to talk to an operator who will look up numbers for you, provided you have the name of the business and town you are looking for. An international operator is available on 155. Calls made from phone boxes are currently free but cost around £0.50 each time from a domestic telephone.

Dial 999 to contact the emergency services—police, fire, ambulance, and mountain rescue services. This number is for emergencies only. The Samaritans offer a 24-hour confidential emotional support for anyone in crisis—0345 909090. Scottish Women's Aid—0131 4752372—offers confidential help to women in crisis.

BUYING YOUR OWN HOME

In Scotland, and Britain in general there is a peculiar mythology that surrounds house ownership. Although most start out their independent lives in rented accommodation, most people aspire one day to actually owning their own property. This is unlike other continental countries such as France where it is normal to take on long term lets rather than actually buying a home.

The reasons are both social and financial. Buying a flat or a house is widely recognised as a prudent investment. After all, why give money away to a landlord when you can pay off a mortgage that will eventually give you your own house instead? Buying property is also considered a good bet because as the value of the house rises with time, so too does the equity in it. Although the housing market is prone to bust as well as boom cycles, property generally appreciates in value, and large profits can be made from buying and selling at the right moment.

Owning your own house is also an important step in life for those who can afford it. It is a measure of sound material progress, that one is moving on in life. In a nation of home lovers, your own flat or house becomes your castle of private seclusion and social respectability.

If someone in Scotland feels financially confident enough to take the plunge and buy a property, they embark on a complex road. The first step is to secure a mortgage from a bank or a building society, as few can afford to pay up front with their own capital.

Mortgages are long-term loans taken out to purchase houses. You can generally get a mortgage of up to three times your salary if you are single, or two and a half times a couple's salary. However this can vary. Whether someone can get a mortgage also depends on employment history and the length and security of their current job.

Some companies also require life insurance to cover themselves in case you drop dead one day. One friend had problems getting life insurance for a mortgage because his medical records showed that he had smoked. You can also be discriminated against if you have been to the doctor for stress or emotional problems. So be wary, as any evidence that you are human or mortal may work against you!

There are a number of different types of mortgages and it is worth shopping around for the best deal. The simplest involve paying off the loan with a set interest in monthly instalments. An Australian mortgage works on the same principle, but calculates the interest daily on the money owed. In theory this means paying less. An endowment mortgage is a form of insurance policy that invests the money you pay in, and at the end of the term you should get a lump sum that equals the amount of your mortgage and, in theory, make a profit as well. There have been problems with these in recent years and it's worth taking financial advice before committing. Most mortgages are repaid over a 25-year period, although this is flexible.

Many Scottish people aspire to own a home, whether it be a house with its own garden, or a small apartment in a block of flats.

Houses are advertised through property magazines or estate agents and solicitors, the middlemen who specialise in buying and selling property. It's best to decide on the area you would like to live in and then scouting around the estate agents, solicitors, and papers local to that area.

The *Solicitor's Property Guide* is a particularly good source as it pools 90% of all properties for sale through solicitors across Scotland. The information is divided up into regions and is available in a weekly publication. The website http://www.espc.co.uk is fast becoming the first port of call if you are buying a home as most estate agents now also advertise on the Internet. Some sites have as many as 75,000 properties for sale at one time, but if they aren't updated regularly, this can become frustrating.

The intrigue starts once you spot the property of your dreams. The seller will have set an asking price, which is usually below what they hope to get for it. Potential buyers then make bids for the house, often well over the asking price when the housing market is going well. Normally they add 10% and then a few thousand on top for good measure. These offers are made independently through solicitors and there is no way of telling how much the others are bidding. After a set deadline has expired, the seller picks the highest offer and the deal is signed and sealed.

The advantage of this very Scottish system is that once the seller has agreed to a price—orally or formally on paper—they are legally committed. They are bound to sell to that person and can't get cold feet and pull out at the last moment without severe penalties. If you have had your bid accepted, this also means that someone else can't cut in with a higher price—known in the trade as guzumping—and snatch the place from under your nose.

This varies sharply with the system in England and Wales. It is filled with uncertainty for both the buyer and seller, an agreed offer that can be reneged on by both parties at any time. It's only when the legal contracts are signed and exchanged by both parties that the deal is set in stone. I have heard of countless horror stories of people who thought they had tied things up only to have the other party pull out hours before the formal papers were due to be signed.

The best way of having a property valued and compared to the seller's asking price is to have a survey carried out. Surveyors value properties and check out potential problems such as damp rot, dry rot, or subsidence. If a surveyor values the property at under the asking price, you can use this to negotiate your offer. A surveyor costs anything from £200 to £300, depending on how thorough the survey is. To check out the competition, you can find out how many other surveys have been made on a property.

At the end of the day the actual value of the property and the number of people interested may have no relation to how much the place is eventually sold for. Markets are vulnerable to many imponderables such as state of the economy, confidence, and fashion. The simplest way of measuring the property market is to read property magazines and compare prices in the area you are interested for comparable properties. Estate agents will also tell you how much previous similar properties have been sold for.

In the past few years house prices have been shooting up in Scotland. Despite a faltering world economy house prices shot up an average of 25% across Great Britain in 2002. Edinburgh has been particularly caught up in the boom, helped by the buzz of a new parliament in the old capital. Property prices in Glasgow have risen apace.

Recently, the asking prices and the value of the property have had little relation to how much they were actually going for. One friend bought a house after months of frustration, losing property after property to people willing to bid way over the asking price. She told me that in one case, the asking price was £123,000, the house was valued at £150,000 and was sold for £175,000!

Such a boom in house prices, over and above inflation, is bound to falter and collapse at some point, as they did at the beginning of the

1990s. The danger in paying a ridiculous price for a house or flat is that if the bubble bursts, you end up with a huge debt and property worth less than what you paid for. This dreaded negative equity was the fate of countless first-time buyers in the early 1990s. Many who lost their work in the general malaise of recession ended up having their homes taken away or repossessed by lenders after failing to meet mortgage payments.

It's worth noting that the cost of buying a house can far exceed what you pay the seller. The solicitor, essential for all the negotiations and legal transactions, will usually charge 1% of the value of the property. However this fee can go up if the value of the property is particularly high. Then there is the fee for the estate agent. There is also a 1% government tax, called a stamp duty, that has to be paid when buying a house or flat.

The Internet is now offering interesting ways of cutting down costs for both buyers and sellers. There are a few companies that offer surveys of houses through the World Wide Web. The idea is that the seller pays to have a survey done which is then put on the net. If you are interested and wish to have a look at the survey, you pay a fee of about £50 to download the report.

SHOPPING

Shops have largely replaced markets in Scotland, with American-style malls increasingly becoming the norm in the cities. There are exceptions, most famously the Barras and Paddy markets in Glasgow where you can pick up any hand-me-down, or electrical goods of unknown origins for a fraction of the retail price.

Little goes to waste in Scotland. Charity shops recycle clothes, books, and other bits and pieces to raise funds for the needy. Oxfam shops are the most famous, but there are plenty of other charity shops that sell stuff that would normally be thrown away. They are a good source of cheap shirts and the occasional bargain, sold at 1940s prices.

Second-hand bookstores are also a great source of pleasure to readers in Scotland. Tucked away in odd corners of towns and cities, they offer hours of dusty browsing in dimly lit labyrinths of shelves and boxes. There are some real gems: For example the tiny bookstore in the village of Blair Atholl holds an impressive array of literature on Scottish myth, legend, and folklore.

There are also plenty of junk shops that sell everything from old radios, bags, door handles, and stuffed animals to the occasional genuine antique. Good deals can be sought privately in the 'for sale' sections of local papers or in car boot sales. A car boot sale is just that, a field where anyone can turn up and sell off their possessions from the boot of their car.

Bargaining or haggling is not the custom in Scotland, or in Britain in general. If something has a price tag on it, that is the price and you are expected to pay it without question. The only exceptions are if you buy something in bulk or offer to pay in cash, in which case it is occasionally possible to arrange some form of discount. It is perfectly acceptable, in fact expected, to drop the price a little in a market, but never more than 20% of the value that's been quoted. The most you can say when hoping to get a price dropped is, "Is this your best price?"

Goods can be bought with cash, cheque, or credit card. Shops and restaurants accept most credit cards. Internet shopping has had a lot of publicity but has yet to take off as an alternative to high street shopping. Concerns over the security of credit card details on the net have yet to be overcome by most consumers.

Clothing measurements are now standardised with the rest of Europe and are in metric.

CULTURAL QUIZ

IF YOU GET THE ANSWER WRONG JIMMY, YOU'LL HAVE TO BUY A ROUND

TRIGG

SITUATION ONE

You mistakenly ask a Scotsman or woman where they come from in England. Do you:

- **A** Apologise profusely.
- **B** Beg for forgiveness.
- **C** Change the subject and hope they didn't hear the question.

Comments

None of the above, as you will be curtly corrected before you can get in a response. The Scots may now have their own parliament and with it a greater sense of self-confidence and separation from England, but they are still touchy when it comes to being confused with the English.

Canadians are so used to being mistaken with Americans when they are abroad that they tend to accept being confused with their Southern neighbours with a mix of grace and weary resignation. The Scots are not so forgiving. It is still common in Scotland to hear "The English" lumped together and derided as being arrogant, insensitive and just about everything else under the sun. So mistakenly calling someone from Scotland English is not a wise move.

Although an English or Scots accent is a pretty reliable marker of identity, it is far from foolproof. There are plenty of well-to-do Scots who lost their accents in private schools in England. And then there are all the immigrants and expatriates who have come back from abroad that further confuse the picture. If in doubt, it is best to assume that everyone in Scotland is Scottish regardless of their accent and wait to see if you are told otherwise. An even worse slip up is to refer to the islands of Great Britain as England. This is enough to make the blood of anyone from Scotland, Wales, or Ireland boil.

SITUATION TWO

You and a friend have gone camping on the west coast of Scotland. It is mid-July and you have walked the long daylight hours until dusk before hurriedly throwing up the tent in the gathering night. You wake up the following morning (your head still brimming from an evening under the stars by the campfire) to the now familiar sound of fine rain on the tent roof. You poke your head out of the tent to inspect the weather only to see a swarm of dancing midges in the still morning air, all eagerly awaiting to make a meal of you. You retreat back into the tent to consider the options. Do you:

A Dive out of the tent regardless; dress, dismantle the tent at speed, and make a quick getaway.

B Perform a delicate contortionist's act to get packed and dressed within the tent, cover every bare patch of skin with insect repellent, and then proceed as above.

C Jump out of the tent and hastily re-light the fire to try and smoke out the midges, thereby buying yourselves time for a more leisurely departure.

D Stay in the tent playing cards for the remainder of the morning. Hopefully, the wind might pick up and blow the midges away, or the sun might break through and send the "wee beasties" back to the ground.

E Don't go camping on the west coast during midge season (between May and September) in the first place.

Comments

Never underestimate a cloud of hungry midges. If you try for the quick getaway you will be virtually eaten alive before you can get the tent pegs out. Covering up and smearing on insect repellent will hold them off only for a while, but not enough to make a clean getaway. Smoke form a fire is of little use unless you are standing directly in its path, risking suffocation.

Waiting for the midges to clear is probably the best option if you have the time. They are at their worst in the mornings and evenings when the light is low and there is little or no breeze. Most canny Scots choose to go camping in the Highlands during early spring or autumn, when colder nights are more than compensated for by the absence of these infuriating wee beasties.

SITUATION THREE

You're in a taxi chatting away to the driver when he completely flummoxes you by asking "Where do you stay?" Do you:

A Tell him what country you're from.

B Tell him where you happen to be staying that night.

C Give him your home address and postcode.

D Tell him the area, town, or city where you are living just now.

E Explain again exactly where you want to be dropped off.

Comments

This common question throws most newcomers in Scotland, including visitors from England, Ireland and Wales. It means, where are you living at the moment? So the correct answer is "C."

SITUATION FOUR

It's Friday night and you have just arrived in a bar with work colleagues for a few drinks. Everyone is in high spirits and eager to make a big night of it. You are happy to stay out with them but don't feel like drinking alcohol. You gingerly approach the bar to be confronted with an array of beers and spirits, as well as a fierce-looking barman waiting for your order. Do you:

A Ask for a half of lemon shandy and explain to your friends and the barman alike that you are feeling a bit peaky.

B Order a coffee and croissant and light up an imported Gittan cigarette with a continental air.

C Ask for "a pint of 80," throw open your wallet and ask what every one else is having. (A "pint of 80" is a bitter brewed by MacEwans called 80 shillings. You will find it in most bars and if you're unsure as to what to have it's a pretty good bet.)

Comments

Answer "C" is what will be expected of you. Pub culture, particularly on weekends, is all about buying rounds of drinks with your mates and generally getting blind drunk with them. Whoever should happen to arrive at the bar first is expected to buy everyone else a drink as well to start the ball rolling.

Women are no exception from the general peer pressure to drink heavily whilst on a big night out. In fact in the spirit of equality between the sexes, women are expected to put down as much booze as the men, and if need be, carry them home at the end of it.

Ordering non-alcoholic shandy on arrival at a bar kind of defeats the object of the whole experience. It will also earn you mild derision from your work colleagues. If you go for the shandy regardless, be ready with a good excuse for you abstinence. Saying you feel unwell isn't enough; you'll end up being plied with that cure-all for every ailment: whisky. The best excuse is to say you have to drive home, even if you only live a stone's throw away from the bar.

Trying to rise above a boozing bar atmosphere by ordering coffee and patisseries is futile. You may as well not go in the first place.

SITUATION FIVE

You have just sat down for a dinner in the house of some new acquaintances, a retired and well-to-do couple called Alasdair and Fiona. This is the first time they have invited you over for a meal and you are keen to make a good impression. Everything is going well until the first course arrives, an inviting bowl of chicken and vegetable soup. It's been a long evening and you are hungry, so after politely waiting for the other guests to serve themselves you smile broadly and tuck in. Moments later Alasdair clears his throat and says, "Let us say grace and thank the Lord for the food we are about to receive." With your soup spoon already firmly lodged in your mouth you will have to act fast to deliver yourself from the disapproval of your God-fearing guests. Do you:

A Say three Hail Mary's and flagellate yourself with what ever comes to hand as penance, hoping that this will bring quick forgiveness before your soup goes cold.

B Wolf down the rest of the soup in time for the last Amen and the second course.

C Mumble an apology, gingerly lick the spoon clean, and lay it back down until Alasdair has finished saying grace.

Comments

Self-flagellation is never a good idea, even in the most desperate of situations. If you continue eating through grace you will be lucky if you even see the second course. The third option is the best one; your pious hosts will take note but won't pass comment until after you have left.

SITUATION SIX

It's Friday night and you have been invited out for a big night on the town. You are to meet in a bar 30 minutes' walk away before moving on to a hot night of clubbing. It's blowing a howling gale outside and the condensation is freezing up on the windows. Taxi or no taxi it's hellish cold out there. Swinging open the wardrobe door you are faced with an array of choices. Do you plum for:

A Thermal underwear, heavy jumpers, two scarves, and wool-lined, tent-shaped long coat.

B A skimpy outfit for club land, natty jacket, and dark glasses.

C Settle for a quiet night by the fire with a mug of cocoa and wait on the spring to venture outside.

Comments

The sensible option is to stay in, although hibernation will do your social life no good. Bundling up in an ill-fitting combination of winter warmers is hardly urban cool, but it will stave off hypothermia. The best option is the most impractical—dress to impress and let the weather take care of itself. Ignoring the cold is the best way to overcome it and if everyone else flounces around in their glad rags in the heart of winter why shouldn't you? Remember that a true Northerner is too hard to notice the cold and that whisky was invented in Scotland to keep you warm as much as to lighten the spirits.

SITUATION SEVEN

You have been invited to your first ceilidh. You desperately want to go but haven't got a clue what to wear and have never danced a Scottish reel in your life. You don't know what the difference is between an eightsome reel and the Charlton, let alone how to negotiate dances like the Duke of Perth and the Gay Gordon. Do you:

A Dash out and buy a book on Scottish reels to practice with the Hoover in front of the mirror. Or find a friend who is in the know and ask them to take you through some of the steps as preparation.

B Politely decline the invitation and stay at home with your two left feet firmly tucked up in a pair of bedroom slippers.

C Throw caution to the wind, go out and hire the full Highland outfit and throw yourself into the melee with more enthusiasm than sense.

Comments

If you decline the invitation you'll needlessly miss out on a great night out. All but the most formal of Scottish ceilidhs are fun and easygoing. The easier reels are quick to pick up and if you take a wrong turn, someone will show you the way. You can always sit out the harder dances and soak up the atmosphere instead of make a complete fool of yourself. Doing your homework beforehand may help but there is no better way to learn than by just turning up and having a go.

However, if you are a novice and go wearing a kilt, you will be expected to know what you are doing. Most ceilidhs have informal dress codes. Jeans and a shirt or T-shirt is fine for boys. Girls often choose to wear summer-style dresses to swirl around in although this is not expected. Of course the Highland balls are considerably more formal affairs.

SITUATION EIGHT

You have been invited for a few days' salmon fishing on the River Tay. Your experience of fishing is stumping around grimy rivers with a can of maggots and a hook and line as a child. You wander into a fish and tackle shop to buy a rod with no idea of what to come away with. Do you opt for:

A A short spinning rod with a combination of bright lures and Day-Glo imitation fish with barbed hooks protruding from their ends (called pugs).

B Settle for what you know and go for the budget option, some line, weights, and a tub seething with maggots or worms.

C Splash out and buy an expensive carbon fibre fly rod with an assortment of feathered flies.

Comments

There is only one correct option for the salmon fisherman or woman in Scotland, the fly rod. You may have no idea of how to wield it and virtually no chance of landing anything larger than stray leaves but that isn't the point. The whole exercise is as much an art as a sport and there is nothing more satisfying than beating the odds to land your first proper fish. There will also be a local gamekeeper, called a ghillie, on hand to show you the ropes. Salmon fishing with a spinner may bring quicker results but it is considered unsporting and is frowned upon. If you appear with worms or maggots you may be mistaken for a poacher and have to beat a hasty retreat from an irate ghillie.

DO'S AND DON'TS APPENDIX

DO'S

- Do be hospitable in your own home. If someone comes to your place, immediately offer them something to drink, be it an electrician fixing the oven or a lifelong friend.
- Be polite and chatty at all times. The Scots are a friendly bunch and like to be acknowledged, so do say, "hello" and ask people how they are regardless of whether they are a friend, someone in a shop or, in more rural areas, just a passerby.
- Do hold eye contact when you shake someone's hand and don't kiss them on the cheek unless you know them well.
- Do watch your language and always be respectful with the elderly. If you are in one of the areas in the Highlands where the Free Church has sway, do strictly observe the Sabbath. This means no work whatsoever on a Sunday— even going for a walk or putting out the washing is frowned upon.
- Do give way to local boy racers and belligerent farmers on single-track roads—they take few prisoners.

- Do give money to the homeless, it's cold out there and they need as much help as they can get.
- If you owe someone money do remember to repay them, they may not remind you but they are unlikely to forget.
- If a formal invitation for a dinner or wedding calls for black tie, do go in a tuxedo and a bow tie rather than a dark suit with a black tie.
- Do say sorry if you bump into someone, not to mention if they bump into you.
- If you are fly fishing do always wear a hat. This isn't as much a question of etiquette as a necessity to avoid ending up with an unwanted ear piercing from an errant cast.
- Do try chips with salt and sauce, haggis, and battered Mars bars, they are all much tastier than they sound!
- Do read *Oor Wullie*, the cartoon adventures of the mischievous wee Glasgow lad in *The Sunday Post*. This much loved cartoon has been running for years and is a great introduction to Scottish humour and the Glasgow patter.

DON'TS

- Don't refuse an offer of a drink in someone else's home, unless you are a good friend or just passing through. This is especially true in the Highlands of Scotland where it is polite to accept the waist-stretching array of biscuits and cake that is often passed to guests. If you are invited to dinner, remember, if possible, to return the invitation within a few weeks.
- Don't catch eyes with groups of young men, particularly if you are a young man yourself. Eye contact, especially on a Friday or Saturday night on the town, can be misinterpreted as a challenge for a fight.
- Don't be afraid to voice your opinions. Apart from formal occasions, you can generally be honest about how you feel

about things, especially politics. However don't open up too quickly about your private life, it takes time to gain true confidence, and tongues may wag in smaller communities.

- Don't interrupt an exchange of pleasantries mid-flow, even if you are in a hurry. There is never too little time for a chat in Scotland.
- Don't photograph people without first asking their permission.
- Don't be offended if you hear swear words, especially in Glasgow where they are often part of the daily patter.
- Don't go and drink in a bar on your own if you are a woman. If you are with a female friend that's fine. Men can, and do, drink alone. If someone includes you in a round of drinks don't order a hugely expensive drink, like a fancy cocktail, unless you are willing to buy the same for every one else when your turn comes round. If someone calls a toast, remember to raise your glass. If someone lightly makes fun of you, laugh rather than take offence; it's all in good humour.
- Don't ask strangers for cigarettes, they are far too expensive in Britain to be given away freely.
- If you wear a kilt don't wear a tartan that you aren't entitled to wear (your parents or grandparents should have the appropriate clan name). Never reveal what you are wearing underneath a kilt, especially if it's nothing.
- Don't claim to be Scottish just because one of your grandparents was.
- Don't make disparaging remarks about Scotland or its people. Scots are fiercely proud of their nation and while they have no problem laughing at themselves, they don't take criticism lightly from foreigners, especially the English.
- Never vocally support English international rugby or football, especially if they are playing Scotland. Supporting an English football league side is OK.
- Don't call whisky bourbon or scotch.

233

GLOSSARY

USEFUL WORDS, PHRASES AND EXPRESSIONS

It is impossible to squeeze into one chapter what could be a lifetime's work. So the following can only be a taster of some of the most commonly used Scots words and expressions.

Introductions

Alright there big man?—Hello there.

Cheerio—Goodbye.

Cheers pal—Can mean thank you or goodbye.

Hiya—Hello.

How'ye you daying/been keeping?—How have you been?

How're you doing?—How are you ?

I'm no bad, and yerself?—I'm OK, how about you?

See you Jimmy/Alright Jimmy—Name given to anyone, being as common as it is. Usually said ironically as it has become such a cliché.

What have you(s) been up tae?—It is common to say "yous" when talking to more than one person.

Where are you fae?—Where are you from?

Where do you bide/ stay—Where are you living just now?

You alright pal?—Are you ok?

The Weather

Haar—East coast sea mist that occasionally comes inland.

It's a grand day—Usually grey but without rain.

Missle/spitting/pishing it down/wet out/dookit—Differing ways of describing rain.

The nights are fair drawing in—It's getting darker earlier.

There's a wee nip in the air—It's cold.

Food and Drink

Bevie (go for a bevy)—An alcoholic drink.

Brekkie—Breakfast.

Fish supper—Fish and chips.

Juice—Describes all soft drinks.

Last orders—"Last orders at the bar" is called just before closing time, giving patrons the chance to get in a last drink. "Time" is shouted when it's time to leave.

Long vodka—Scottish cocktail which mixes vodka, lime, tonic water and angostura bitters.

Piece—Sandwich.

Pished/guttered/smashed/reekin/fleain/absolutly steamin'—These terms are used to describe varying levels of intoxication.

Pokey hat—99 flake ice cream.

Scran—Food.

Tea/supper—Dinner.

The Land

Ben—Hill.

Black house—Thick-walled traditional house.

Bothy—Shepherds mountain shelter.

Brae—Slope, hill.

Brig—Bridge.

Burn—Stream.

Cairn—Pile of stones at the peak of hills and mountains.

Corrie—Smaller valley between hills.

Croft—Small cottage and area of land.

Dolmen—Grave chamber.

Dyke—Old stone division of land.

Glen—Valley.

Inch—Small island.

Kirk—Church.

Kyle—Narrow strait or channel.

Lazy bed—Old crofting system of agriculture still maintained in areas such as the Outer Hebrides. The thin soil has poor drainage. To improve the soil's productivity, vegetable patches are raised and laid over with seaweed, manure and thatch for fertiliser. The channels between them provide drainage.

Links—Land running next to the sea.

Loch—Lake.

Lochan—Mini lake.

Manse—Official house of a presbyterian minister.

Moor—Open plane.

Runrig—A system by which rural communities would rotate their corps, sharing out the land and it's resources and ensuring that no one area was over cultivated. Runrig is also the name of a monumental eighties Scottish rock band.

Strath—Broad, flat river valley.

Gaelic Place Names

The individual names of places in Gaelic don't just sound good to the ear. They offer up wisdom on the significance that earlier people gave to their local area. Translate local place names and an unseen world opens up; where language, place, history and identity becomes bonded in light and stone. Take some of the names around the central highland town of Pitlochry as an example. The following is a translation of some of the local land marks.

Ben-y-Vrackie—The speckled mountain named after the white flashes of quarts on the mountain, now long since quarried.

Craigower—The goats tower.

Faskally—The resting place in the wood.

Fonab—Abbots' land.

Loch Tummel—Lake of the hot stream.

Killiecrankie—Wood of the aspen tree.

Moulin—Smooth, rounded hill.

Pitlochry—Comes from a mix of Pictish and Gaelic. It means "The place of the sentinel stone" (pit-cloich-aire). it is speculated that the town marks an old guarding place for the Picts against the Romans.
Port-na-Craig—Ferry by the rock. The rock is still in the river Tummel, although the ferry has long since has long since been replaced by a suspension bridge.

Words and Phrases

Aye—"Aye" means *yes* and much more. It can be used as a short and crisp affirmative or a drawn out to give agreement to a point of discussion. It can simply be said to gently fill a silence. Old boys in bars punctuate lulls in conversation with the occasional "aye."

A good crack/a real hoot—A good time.

A widnae mis um an hit the wa—I've got the hots for him.

Bag off—To kiss.

Bairn—Baby.

Barry—Good (Edinburgh term).

Blether—To talk.

Boaby—Penis.

Boggin—Revolting.

Bonnie—Beautiful.

Burik—A mess.

Go for a burn—To go for a fast drive or cycle.

By the way—Used all the time as punctuation in speech.

Chancer—Someone who is sly or opportunistic.

Chum—To keep company with: "Chum tae the shop."

Curls your teeth—Tastes horrible.

Do you ken?—Do you understand/know?

Dram—Measure of whisky.

Dricht—Wet and miserable weather.

Earn you keep—Pay your way.

Feart—Fear.

Fine fettle—In good form.

Fluke—Lucky break.

Folk—People.

Fucking cracked it!—To finish or overcome something.

Gagy—Boy or man.

Greet—To cry ("Stop yur greeting").

Galore—Gaelic word meaning "enough."

Gimme two secs—I'll be with you in a second.

Glasgow kiss—Head butt.

Heebie jeebies—Scared.

Hen—Woman.

Hummin—Smells really bad.

I don't have a scoobie—I have no idea.

I've got the glass on you—I've been watching you (a Highland phrase).

Jiggered—Exhausted.

Jock—Mildly derogatory term for a Scot. However the Scots call each other jock.

Lass—Woman.

Mac—Son of.

Mackle—Big.

Mental—Crazy. It's common to say "totally mental."

Mingin—Disgusting.

Muckle /peedie—Small. Peedie is an Orkney word.

Nay bother—Don't worry/no problem.

Nips your head/a wee bit nippy—Something that is frustrating.

Off the sauce—Not drinking alcohol.

Old reekie—Edinburgh.

Pal—Friend.

Radge—Foul.

Sair—Sore.

Soon faced—Glum.

Sassenach—Southerner.

Shuftie—To have a quick look at something.

Skeemie—Someone who lives in one of the poor housing estates or "schemes."

Skelp—To smack or hit.

Sketchy—Dubious.

Sleakit—Someone who is sly.

Spare prick at a wedding—Standing out, not fitting in.

Spawney—Lucky.

Snooty—Pretentious.

Stour—Dust.

Swithering—Wracked with indecision.

The pictures—The movies.

That's champion—That's brilliant.

The wiege—Glasgow.

Dinnae hav the willies—Don't get scared.

To have the glad eye—To fancy someone.

Toonie—Someone from a town or city.

Wee—Small.

What er ye like—What are you like.

Whitie—Moment of total panic.

Wing it—To get through a difficult situation by chance alone.

Workies—Builders.

Jakey—Alcoholic or junkie.

Yen—Man.

Yer ma—I don't believe you.

You beauty/oh ya fucking beautie—Fantastic!

You must be joking—You can't be serious.

Work

Admin—Administration.

AGM—Annual General Meeting.

F/t—Full-time

HQ—Headquarters.

HR—Human Resources.

IT—Information Technology.
MD—Managing Director
P/t—Part-time
PA—Personal Assistant
PR—Public Relations
Temp—Temporary Worker

Addresses

Av—Avenue
C/o—Care of
Cres—Crescent
F—Flat
GB—Great Britain
Gdns—Gardens
Nr—Near
PO box—Post Office box
Rd—Road
UK—United Kingdom

Politics

Green—Green Party
Lab—Labour Party
MSP—Minister of the Scottish Parliament
SNP—Scottish National Party
SWP—Scottish Workers' Party

CALENDAR OF FESTIVALS AND HOLIDAYS

This can only be a brief and inadequate guide to the biggest events in the Scottish calendar. Every city town and village has its own round of festivals and traditions which are best sought out locally.

December 31—Hogmanay! This was originally an old Celtic festival to hasten back the sun, and until recently was more important than Christmas. It's now a massive knees-up held to usher in the New Year.

In the countryside, the tradition called "first-footing" means that homes are thrown open, and the first visit, or first foot, across the door of a friend's house after the beginning of the New Year is celebrated with a drink of whisky all round. The tradition is most prevalent in the smaller communities where a whole village circulates from one home to the next having an alcoholic drink in each until the early hours and often days beyond. I once went round to visit the Kennedy family a few days after the New Year in Perthshire. John Kennedy asked me if I would like a drink and I said I'd love a cup of tea. "Would you like a drink with your cup of tea?" came the reply.

Traditionally, visitors would bring a piece of coal symbolising warmth for the hearth, as well as whisky, when they entered a house for the first time after a New Year. My family once had to delay a trip to England by a whole week because my parents were first-footing a bit too enthusiastically. Each day they woke unable to face the drive, and had to put it off once again.

In the towns and cities you can drop by at most parties regardless of whether or not you know anyone, and expect a warm welcome. It is also tradition to kiss anybody of the opposite sex that you happen to bump into, so remember to take lots of lip balm. It is a wonderful open-hearted and joyful celebration.

Although Hogmanay is technically just the one night of celebration, it generally turns into a two-week binge of eating and drinking from Christmas until around the January 6. When folk get tired of the theme of ushering in the New Year, they carry right on celebrating just for the sake of it. The only way to get through such sustained festivities is to stay on the alcohol, a steady flow to hold off the hangover till you make it back to the normal world again.

January 25—Burns Night. A celebration of Scotland's principal Bard (poet). The poet Robert Burns has an enduring reputation in Scotland. An instinctive rebel just when the French Revolution was throwing over the old guard, he brought a breath of fresh air to the stifling social constraints of late 18th century. With a swashbuckling, boozing lifestyle and breathtaking skill with words—he is reputed to have written the famous poem *Tam O'Shanter* in a day—Burns has captured the popular imagination ever since.

Burns Night is quintessentially Scottish in character. For one evening those who care to, bring out the old clichés and get dewy-eyed about this sharpest and most sentimental of bards. In doing so, a little like the Australian Aborigines in Bruce Chatwin's book *Song Lines*, they sing their imagined community back into existence every year.

Burns Night is a social occasion, when friends gather to eat haggis, tatties, and neeps and drink a wee dram or two to Burns' dear departed ghost. The night is also filled with ritual. The haggis is traditionally brought to the table accompanied by a piper playing traditional tunes on the bagpipes, where Burns' *An Ode to the Haggis* is read out to much applause.

After the meal it is time for the speeches. *The Immortal Memory* is the most important attempt to eulogise Burns' life and achievements. There is much room for interpretation here as little is actually known about the man himself. The male guests are also given free reign to compose a *Tribute to the Lassie*, and the women then come up with the *Lassies' Reply*. These poems certainly lack the lyricism of Robbie Burns and are often smutty and raucous. Not that Burns would have minded—he is known to have been a veritable Don Juan of the north himself.

The form speeches take is far from rigid. The "Tribute to the Lassie" can be a tribute to almost anything. I have heard tributes to agriculture and whisky. At the Burns Night held by the Scottish Labour Party, satirical poems were scribed for both the parliament in Westminster and the new Edinburgh equivalent.

Although many celebrate Burns Night in Scotland, the romance of the night holds a stronger pull outside the country. In North America the tradition has really taken off amongst the countries' Celtic descendants. Clubs such as the well-to-do Caledonian Club in New York hold huge society dinners with upwards of two hundred guests. Even the desert state of Nevada, a far cry from the rainswept mountains of the Highlands, boasts a Cold Country Celtic Society. The society holds a huge party complete with pipers, Scottish dancing, and a free bar (unheard of in Scotland) on the night of the 25th.

In London or New York, the pubs and bars often give out haggis and whisky on Burns Night as the Scots émigrés or their descendants reminisce about their old country. In the bars of the main cities in Scotland, it's business as usual and the dinners themselves tend to be much more intimate affairs of family and friends. However this doesn't mean that Burns is forgotten.

January—Shetland Islands "Up Helly Aa" festival. This two-week festival celebrates the Isles' Old Norse heritage and ends with the traditional burning of a Viking longship and a torchlight procession through the streets of Lerwick.

February 14—St Valentine's Day. A chance to send anonymous cards filled with love or lust to long-term partners and potential suitors. This is a particularly charged day at school with kids comparing cards, trying to guess who sent them and seeing who got the most.

May 1—International Workers Day, known as May Day. Big processions are held in the cities—the largest in Glasgow—to show solidarity with workers across the globe.

May 1—Beltane Fire Festival. Traditionally a Celtic fire festival to celebrate the Celtic New Year. There has been a revival of the festival on Carlton Hill in Edinburgh in recent years in which thousands gather to see the May Queen and the Green Man triumph against the forces of winter. Many towns and villages across the country still light big bonfires on high points after nightfall. In ancient times, Celtic druids believed the dew before dawn on the morning after Beltane was sacred. Many still wash their faces in this dew on Arthur's Seat in Edinburgh in the hope that it will give them eternal youth.

March/April—Easter. The Christian celebration of Jesus' resurrection. The date varies as it depends on the phases of the moon rather than the solar calendar.

Like most of the religious festivals in Scotland, Easter has pre-Christian origins. The word "Easter" also comes from the Celtic goddess of light and spring. The tradition of giving chocolate Easter eggs, symbolising new life, dates back to older pagan spring festivals.

In an increasingly secular society the religious significance of Easter is less important than it used to be. It is first and foremost a public holiday, running from Good Friday to Easter Monday.

April 1—April Fool's Day. April Fool's is worth mentioning as it has caught out many an unsuspecting visitor. Called "hunt the gowk" in Scots (the nearest translation is "fool"), the first of April is a day for people to play practical jokes on each other. These jokes can be very elaborate. Back in the 1970s the British Broadcasting Corporation (BBC), duped the entire nation by running a documentary on Italian spaghetti farming, complete with footage of the farmers picking strands of pasta off spaghetti "trees."

Spring—Common Riding/Riding of the Marches. This is a uniquely Scottish practice where the inhabitants of local areas ride out to the perimeters of their old "burghs" to assert their identity. The dates and ceremonies, such as mock battles, vary from town to town but most of the common riding is on the borders with England. The

Selkirk Riding commemorates the Battle of Flodden back in 1513 against the English.

July 12—The Orange Marches. Held in Glasgow, the Protestant Orange Order marches through town to remind the Catholics who's in charge.

August/September—The Highland Games. The most famous games are held at Aboyne, Braemar, Glenfinnan, Inverness and Crieff (see chapter eight).

August 10–30—The Edinburgh Festival. Europe's biggest arts festival includes theatre, comedy, dance, music, film, literature, military tattoos, and more. Be sure to find accommodation well ahead of time, the city gets so crowded that it's hard enough finding six feet of floor space, let alone a bed!

October 31—Halloween. Halloween is the night before the old church festival of All Hallows, or All Saints' Day. This is also an important date in the Celtic calendar, Samhuinn the Feast of the Dead, during which spirits are said to come back to haunt the living. Samhuinn holds more appeal with the young who hollow out pumpkins, cut with grotesque faces to scare away the dead.

Witches were said to be very active during Samhuinn. They still are, in the form of kids that go out dressed up as ghouls, witches, and apparitions to demand sweets from their neighbours. Called trick-or-treating elsewhere in the world, it's called "Guising" in Scotland. Originally, the Guisers had to sing or recite a poem to earn their reward of sweets, but now the costumes are enough. The trick, such as a fireworks through the letterbox, can be real if people are unfriendly and don't hand over sweets.

November 5—Guy Faulkes Night. A Britain-wide celebration of Guy Faulkes' death. Guy Faulkes was a 17th century anarchist who almost blew up the Houses of Parliament in London by stacking its basement with gunpowder. He was caught before he could ignite the fuse and burned at the stake, an event remembered with bonfires, the burning of effigies of "The Guy" and lots of fireworks.

The Scots have an ambiguous relationship with Guy Faulkes. Whereas in England, the night is a celebration of a catastrophe narrowly avoided, many in Scotland are more inclined to celebrate his near success. In truth, the events of the time are largely forgotten and it is more of an excuse to gather around a big bonfire on a chilly night, wave sparklers, set off fireworks, and drink spirits to keep warm.

November 30—St Andrew's Day. Scotland's national day and an occasion for the Scots to celebrate their patron saint Andrew.

December 25—Christmas, celebrating the birth of Jesus. Christmas comes early in Scotland. From the middle of November the shops start decking themselves out in tinsel and fake snow, preparing for the shopping onslaught as everyone goes hunting for presents.

The pubs fill up in the days running up to Christmas and the restaurants do a roaring trade hosting a seemingly endless round of work parties. It is also a time for amorous advances and minor indiscretions. So if someone approaches you with a sprig of a plant with white berries around Christmas, brace yourself. It's mistletoe and tradition has it that whoever stands under it has to kiss.

Christmas is also an important time to get in touch with friends and family. It is customary to give a Christmas card to practically everyone you know. Most people spend the big day itself with their family. St Nicholas, or Santa Claus, pops down chimneys to fill big stockings at the end of children's beds with presents the night before. Presents are also laid out under the Christmas tree and traditionally opened after lunch, if everyone can wait that long. Christmas dinner is a huge feast of turkey, vegetables, and roast potatoes. Christmas Mass is most commonly held at midnight before December 25.

RESOURCE GUIDE

The following list of Internet sites should quench the most insatiable of thirsts for information on Scotland. I have chosen more established sites that are regularly updated and unlikely to disappear overnight into the virtual ether.

EMERGENCIES AND HEALTH
National Health System (NHS)
http://www.nhs50.nhs.uk
400 pages of information, history, and advice from the heart of Britain's welfare state.

The Health Education Board of Scotland (HEBS)
http://www.hebs.org.uk
A wealth of useful information on how best to avoid illness.

Heal Self
http://www.healself.com
An alternative take on conventional medicine. Offers information on everything from organic food to alternative therapies.

Disabled Information
http://www.disabledinfo.com
A comprehensive database of information for disabled people, with good links to other relevant sites.

HOME AND FAMILY
Property Live
http://www.propertylive.co.uk
Quick access to approved estate agents across Britain.

Homes Online
http://www.hol365.com
Renting or buying this a good place to start.

Scottish Solicitors Property Centres
http://www.sspc.co.uk
Information of properties to rent or buy from solicitors is pooled on this site. From the homepage page you can click through to see properties in any part of Scotland.

Scottish Tourist Board Official Website
http://www.visitscotland.com
This Scottish Tourist Board site gives a good list of places to stay while you are exploring Scotland.

Youth Hostels Association
http://www.yha.org.uk
One of the best budget options for touring Scotland on a shoestring.

Department for Education and Skills
http://www.dfee.gov.uk
A massive information source that includes school performance tables, and a guide to finance for prospective university students.

Universities and Colleges Admissions Service for the UK (UCAS)
http://www.ucas.ac.uk
Everything you wanted to know about choosing and getting into higher education in the UK but were afraid to ask.

MANAGING YOUR MONEY
The Inland Revenue
http://www.inlandrevenue.gov.uk
The official source on all your tax needs, you can even fill in your tax forms here online.

Internet Banking
http://www.internet-banking.com
General information on Internet banking.

The Royal Bank of Scotland
http://www.rbs.co.uk
All the high street banks have websites that will help answer any general questions. This is just one example.

ENTERTAINMENT AND LEISURE
Scotland's Internet Directory
http://www.scotland.org
Boasts over 7,000 links to theatre, music, cinema, and much more!

Edinburgh Festivals

http://www.go-edinburgh.co.uk

A good source of festival information for the city's summer madness.

Shopsmart

http://uk.shopsmart.com/

One of the UK's leading online shopping portals.

Film Finder

http://search.yell.com/search/FilmSearch

Type in the cinema locations closest to you and find out what's showing at the local cinemas.

UK Theatre Web

http://www.uktw.co.uk

Keep abreast of what's going on in the world of theatre with this fun, informal site.

Book Wire

http://www.bookwire.com

Latest authors gossip and reviews from the UK book industry's No. 1 source of information.

Amazon

http://www.amazon.co.uk

Order books, CDs, DVDs, or even household appliances and outdoor furniture online.

TRANSPORT AND COMMUNICATIONS

UK Travel

http://www.uktravel.com

Good general information on everything from visas, car hire, and ferries to good eateries and places to stay along the way.

Cheap Flights

http://www.cheapflights.co.uk

This website pools cheap deals and offers and is a good place to shop around for bargains.

Ryan Air

http://www.ryanair.com

On-line booking site for cheap flights in and around the UK.

GO

http://www.go-fly.co.uk

Cheap flights around Europe, including Edinburgh to London.

Eurostar

http://www.eurostar.com

For express travel by train from London to Paris you can book on-line at Eurostar's website.

Railtrack Travel Information

http://www.railtrack.co.uk

The UK's major train operators offer up-to-date train information on this site.

Ferrybooker

http://www.ferrybooker.com

The most comprehensive of on-line booking sites for passage by sea to or from the British Isles.

Caledonian MacBrayne

http://www.calmac.co.uk

This is the site for most ferry crossings to the small isles in Scotland. You can book your tickets from here in advance. The website also has links to tour operators offering holiday packages.

National Express
http://www.gobycoach.com
For travel by coach between principal cities in Scotland and the UK.

Driver and Vehicle Licensing Agency
http://www.dvla.gov.uk/
For all information on driving licences, including how to get an international driving permit from abroad.

The Automobile Association (AA)
http://www.theaa.com/
A comprehensive site for drivers, including maps, travel information, hotel guide, and quick insurance quotes.

Royal Automobile Association (RAC)
http://www.rac.co.uk
More good information and advice for motorists.

EasyMap
http://www.easymap.co.uk
Find the exact location of any address in the country, or map out your own route through Scotland on this user-friendly website.

MEDIA
BBC News
http://news.bbc.co.uk
Catch the breaking stories on this pioneering site by the British Broadcasting Corporation, better known as the BBC or the "beeb."

Scottish Media Links
http://www.geo.ed.ac.uk/home/scotland/media.html
The Gateway to Scotland site has this link page to all the major Scottish newspapers as well as Scottish television.

LANGUAGE
The British Council in Scotland
http://www.britishcouncil.org/scotland/english/index.htm
The cream, and also the most expensive, of the English language schools in Scotland.

RELIGION AND SOCIAL WORK
The Church of Scotland
http://www.churchofscotland.org.uk/

The Free Church of Scotland
http://www.freechurch.org

The Catholic Encyclopaedia
http://www.newadvent.org

The Hindu Universe
http://www.hindunet.org

The Islamic Digest
http://www.islamicdigest.org

The Muslim News
http://www.muslimnews.co.uk

Astrology
http://www.astrology.net
The on-line bible for new age spiritualists.

GENERAL COUNTRY INFORMATION
Gateway to Scotland
http://www.geo.ed.ac.uk/home/scotland/scotland.html
A wealth of general information and links on Scotland.

Rampant Scotland Directory
http://www.rampantscotland.com
A quick way to hunt for information on Scotland, however bizarre.

British Politics Page
http://www.ukpol.co.uk
A good starting point for learning about politics in Scotland and Great Britain. This site has over 15,000 links to other political web-pages.

Scottish Executive
http://www.scotland.gov.uk/default.asp
Read about the ins and outs of the Scottish parliament, and keep up-to-date with breaking stories.

Home Office
http://www.homeoffice.gov.uk
Government site complete with visa and immigration information.

The Department of Social Security
http://www.dss.gov.uk/
UK government agency offering benefits advice and general information on what is available for the financially challenged.

Citizens Advice Bureaux (CAB)
http://www.nacab.org.uk
Free advice on anything from housing to immigration law. The Citizens Advice Bureaux has offices in most cities and towns.

BUSINESS INFORMATION
Scottish Enterprise Network
http://www.scottish-enterprise.com
Good information on business advice, news and networking opportunities in Scotland

UK Directory
http://www.ukdirectory.com
A comprehensive database of business related websites in the UK.

The London Stock Exchange
http://www.londonstockexchange.com/
Follow the ups and downs of the stock market from the comfort of
your own PC.

FURTHER READING

Journeys Through Time and Place

Samuel Johnson and James Boswell's *A Journey to the Western Isles of Scotland* and *The Journal of a Tour to the Hebrides* (Penguin, 1999) is the most famous account of a journey round the islands. Another classic Scottish travelogue is Edwin Muir's *Scottish Journey* (Mainstream, 1999). Written in 1935, it covers much of Scotland before the Second World War. But it isn't dated; the landscapes, people and social commentary offer lasting echoes of Scotland today.

R. F. Mackenzie's *A Search for Scotland* (Fontana) is more of a very personal trip into Mackenzie's own cultural roots, touching on most aspects of Scots culture with a wry and sometimes critical eye. The book is currently out of print but is easy to pick up in a library or second hand bookshop.

David Craig's *On the Crofters' Trail* (Pimlico, 1999) is the best modern account of the Highland Clearances, told through interviews with descendants.

For a broad taste of travel writing, both new and old, try *The Road North: 300 Years of Classic Scottish Travel Writing* (The In Pinn, 2000). Edited by June Skinner Sawyers, *The Road North* has extracts from the likes of T.S. Eliot, Gavin Maxwell and Niel Gunn.

History and Politics

The best all-round history book has to be *Scotland: A New History* (Pimlico, 1992) by Michael Lynch. Lynch manages the impossible; to compress a broad narrative of Scots history since the times of Picts into one volume.

J. D. Mackie's *A History of Scotland* (Penguin, 1991) is another good study that doesn't get too bogged down in details.

For more in-depth studies on certain aspects of Scottish history, John Prebble stands head and shoulders above the rest. He wrote captivating books on the massacre of Glencoe, Culloden, and the Highland clearances (Penguin) back in the 1960s and 1970s. He has recently published a more personal reflection on the country and it's troubled history called *Scotland Road Trip* (Pimlico, 2000).

Historic Scotland (Stationery Office/Seven Mills) publishes a whole range of cheerful guides on Scotland's history and prehistory, complete with stunning photographs. Their guide to Scotland's castles is particularly good.

T. C. Smout's *A History of the Scottish People 1830–1950* (Fontana Press, 1997) offers a great social history of the time complete with old black and white photographs.

A good way to understand more about Scotland's old feudal society is to read up on clan history. Here there is a massive choice. *Collins Clans and Tartans* (Collins, 1999) gives a good, if brief, history. Donald Whyte's *Scottish Surnames and Families* (Burlin, 2000) is much more in depth. For a contemporary outlook on

Scotland's continued feudal system of land ownership, Andy Wightman's *Who Owns Scotland* (Canongate, 2000) has become a classic reference book for those calling for reform.

Modern day reflections on the new era of political devolution are still a little thin on the ground as the project is still very fresh. For a detailed analysis try *The New Scottish Politics—The First Year of the Scottish Parliament and Beyond* (The Stationery Office, 2000), edited by Gerry Hassan and Chris Warhurst.

Myth and Legend

Scottish Fairy and Folk Tales (General Publishing Company, 2000), edited by Sir George Douglas is a reprint of a centuries old classic. The Scots can be difficult to digest in places but the stories themselves are captivating. For a more modern and slightly more academic approach to clan lore, witchcraft and other superstitions, *The Folklore of the Scottish Highlands* (Tempus, 2000) by Anne Ross is excellent. UFO aficionado Ron Halliday's book *The A-Z of Paranormal Scotland* (Black and White Publishing, 2000) is an entertaining read if you are into ghost stories.

Language

The Essential Guide to Modern Scots (HarperCollins, 1996) is a good guide to Scots phrases and accents. For more extensive coverage the *Concise Scots Dictionary* (Polygon, 2000) is also very good. Glasgow has a particularly fast and entertaining dialect and *The Complete Patter* (Canongate, 1996) by Michael Munro does it justice.

Scottish Gaelic in Three Months (Hugo, 1999) covers basic pronunciation, vocabulary and grammar in step-by-step lessons. Malcolm MacLennan's *Gaelic Dictionary* (Acair & Mercat Press, 1992) is a good reference work.

Scotland's Place Names (Mercat Press, 1998) by David Dorward makes easy sense of many of the Gaelic place names without turning them into a long list.

Guides

Bookstores in Scotland are littered with guides. The ubiquitous *Lonely Planet* and *Rough Guide* series are the best known for all-round travel information. Both are pretty comprehensive and regularly updated. Another very popular buy is *Scotland the Best: The One True Guide* (HarperCollins, 2000), by Peter Irvine.

Good bets for a quirkier look at Scotland's principle cities are Moira Burgess' *Reading Glasgow* (Book Trust Scotland, 1999) and *The Literary Companion to Edinburgh* (Methuen, 2000) by Andrew Lowne.

Outdoor Pursuits

Guides for walkers and climbers are plentiful. For climbing Scotland's Munros, a good coffee table book is *The Munros – Scotland's Highest Mountains* (Lomond Books, 2000) by Cameron McNeish. Filled with detail, maps and photographs of the 248 mountains over 3000 meters in Scotland, some of the proceeds from sales are also donated to the Mountain Rescue Service. A better pocket companion is Cameron McNeish's *The Munro Almanac* (Interlink Publishing, 2000).

There are a number of more general walkers' guides that cover the whole of Scotland. For more practical information, *Pathfinder Guides* (Ordnance Survey-Jarrold, 1999) have clearly laid out maps with colour coded routs. Ordinance Survey also produces the most detailed maps of the whole of the British Isles designed for orienteering with a compass.

Some of the most popular walks have whole books devoted to them. For example *The West Highland Way* (Mercat Press, 2000) by Bob Aitken and Roger Smith includes local history and photos along the way.

If you need contact details, ratings and reviews on Golf courses a good bet is *Golf World – The Best Courses in Scotland* (Aurum, 2000) A more comprehensive companion is the *AA Guide to Golf Courses UK* (AA Publishing, 2000) which includes listings of places to stay.

Food and Drink

Scots Cooking by Sue Lawrence (Headline Books, 2000) gives quick immersion into Scots cuisine with both traditional and modern recipes, together with mouthwatering photos. For a more extensive handbook, Catherine Brown's *Scottish Cooking* (Redwood Books, 1999) is superb. It covers everything from home baking to the lifestyles and cooking times of wild game.

The Whisky Trails (Prion Books, 2000) by Gordon Brown gives a comprehensive and up-to-date guide to the distilleries trail, including information on other nearby sites of local interest. For a more definitive guide on all aspects of whisky, read Michael Jackson's *Malt Whisky Companion* (Dorling Kindersley, 2000).

Picture Books

Colin Baxter has something of a monopoly on landscape photography in Scotland, not surprising when no one can come close to his brooding images of mood and light. *Scotland–Photos by Colin Baxter* (1998) is a good example. For the people side of Scotland, *Scotland's Century—1900–2000* (Lomond Books, 2000) is full of striking images. Oscar Marzaroli's *Shades of Scotland 1959-1988* (British Library, 1989) is an another classy mix of portraits and landscape.

The Scottish House—Eclectic and Unique Interiors (Collins and Brown, 2000) is a sumptuous collection of photos of the insides of various stately homes, lodges and castles by Ianthe Ruthven.

General

The *Encyclopaedia of Scotland* (Collins, 2000), newly revised and updated by editors Julia Keay and John Keay, is an awesome reference book on everything you wanted to know about Scotland but were afraid to ask. For hard data, *Whitaker's Almanack 2001* (The Stationery Office, 2000) is packed with information and useful addresses.

THE AUTHOR

 Born in Inverness in 1970, Jamie Grant spent many years as a boy living in a small village on the west coast of Scotland. Here he learnt the subtle arts of stone-throwing and jellyfish-stamping long before he heard of the likes of Flora Macdonald or the colourists.

His total immersion in all things Scottish came later in life. After going to university in Cardiff, he spent the best part of his twenties in South America, working as an English teacher, journalist and photographer. Whilst nearly drowning in an Amazon river, he had a vision of his distant homeland and decided to make the long pilgrimage back to Scotland. On return he found everything he had dreamt of and nothing he had expected. Jamie now lives and writes in Scotland.

INDEX